simply italian

simply italian

Ruth Glick

SURREY BOOKS

Chicago

SIMPLY ITALIAN
is published by Surrey Books, Inc.
230 E. Ohio St., Suite 120, Chicago, IL 60611

First Edition 1 2 3 4 5

This book is manufactured in the United States of America

Library of Congress Cataloging-in-Publication Data

Glick, Ruth, 1942–

    Simply Italian / Ruth Glick.—1st ed.
      p. cm.
    Includes index.
    ISBN 1-57284-022-6 (pbk.)
    1. Cookery, Italian. 2. Low-fat diet—Recipes. 3. Salt-free diet—Recipes.
    4. Low-calorie diet—Recipes. I. Title.
    TX723.G624   1999
    641.5945—dc21   98-39487
                    CIP

Illustrations © 1999 Patti Green
Editorial and production: Bookcrafters, Inc., Chicago
Design and typesetting: Joan Sommers Design, Chicago
Nutritional analyses: Linda R. Yoakam, M.S., R.D.

For free catalog and prices on quantity purchases, contact Surrey Books
at the address above

This title is distributed to the trade by Publishers Group West

As always, I want to thank my husband Norman Glick, who is both a great editor and eater. I also want to thank Nancy Baggett for helping me with recipe development. Joe Galitsky tested many of these recipes in my kitchen. Binnie Braunstein also helped with editing and was one of my most valued tasters, as were the members of the Columbia Writers Workshop.

contents

introduction

Italian cooking, with its rich tradition of regional specialties and classic dishes, is one of the great cuisines of the world. It's also an American favorite. Witness the popularity of pastas and pizzas in their infinite variety; thick, hearty soups such as minestrone; and that darling of the dessert cart, tiramisu.

Italian cooks had a head start on culinary sophistication. Roman citizens were dining at opulent banquets when most of the world's inhabitants were still charring antelope over open fires. And the great city-states of the Renaissance were as famous for their dining pleasure as for their art treasures.

Today we still want the same wonderful dishes and flavor combinations that have been handed down through generations of Italian kitchens. But few of us have the time or the energy for a long session in front of the stove after a hard day's work.

That's why I've written *Simply Italian*, a book that translates this great culinary tradition into simpler terms that every American cook can adapt. In these pages you'll find a classic variety of flavorful ingredients: herbs and spices such as oregano, thyme, basil, garlic, and parsley; tomatoes; Parmesan, mozzarella, and ricotta cheese; sausage; and olive oil—all staples of Italian cooking for hundreds of years. Many are fresh ingredients you can quickly turn into tempting dishes. Others are in more convenient form: flavored sauces, grated cheeses, minced garlic, frozen vegetable mixtures, premade pizza shells, and pasta from the dairy case that make life much easier for the modern cook.

Many of the dishes in this recipe collection can be on the table in 30 minutes or less, some with the assistance of the microwave (a 900-watt unit was used to develop these recipes). Others take a bit more cooking time so flavors can develop, but each recipe tells you right up front how much preparation and cooking time to expect. All of the recipes are easy, and many come with helpful hints to speed your progress.

There's even a chapter of extra-quick, prèsto, dishes such as Fresh Basil-Parsley Sauce with Fettuccine, Chicken Caesar Sandwich, and Sausage and Peppers Sauce that go on the table in a snap.

As you look through the book, you may also notice another plus. Many of the recipes are modified so that they're lower in fat than the original Italian versions. I've always been a health-conscious cook, and I take advantage of ingredients that weren't available in my mother's day. For example, instead of using full-fat dairy products like ricotta and mozzarella cheese and sour cream, I've substituted their reduced-fat counterparts where taste and texture would not be affected. And I've often reduced the oil or butter in dishes where larger amounts aren't really needed for rich and flavorful results.

Every recipe includes a nutritional analysis done by a registered dietitian using the latest professional nutritional analysis software. You can see at a glance exactly how many calories and how much fat, saturated fat, cholesterol, sodium, protein, dietary fiber, and carbohydrates are in each serving.

Remember that the nutritional analyses are not infallible. Many factors can affect their accuracy: variability in the size of the produce; variability in weights and measures; a plus or minus 20 percent error factor in labeling prepared foods; and variations in personal cooking methods.

Where a range of serving sizes is given, the analysis is based on the larger number of servings. When a choice of ingredients is given, (for example, chicken broth *or* vegetable broth; reduced-sodium *or* regular tomato sauce), the analysis is based on the first choice. If a quantity range is given (for example, 3–4 ounces pepperoni), the analysis is based on the first number. Optional, "to taste," and ingredients identified as garnishes are not included in the analyses.

Simply Italian covers a whole range of wonderful foods—everything from Broiled Portobello Mushrooms and Hearty Minestrone with Pepperoni to classic Marinara Sauce, Grilled Beef and Peppers, Salmon Risotto, Roasted Vegetables, and Pepperoni Pizza. Along with the main and side dishes is a wonderful selection of easy Italian desserts such as Fruit Pizza, Zuppa Inglese, Pear-Almond Cake, and Lemon Granita. Try some of these tempting dishes, and you'll find how simple it is to modify Italian cooking for today's tastes and lifestyles—without sacrificing the wonderful flavors of this classic cuisine.

CONVENIENT INGREDIENTS

Over the years I've found that a number of convenience foods make life a lot easier for the busy cook. Here are the ones I keep in my own kitchen and used to prepare the recipes in *Simply Italian.*

Artichoke Hearts The distinctive flavor of artichokes permeates many Italian dishes. If you had to start with the fresh vegetable, you'd spend a great deal of preparation time. However, you can buy artichoke hearts in cans and jars and conveniently use them in salads, appetizers, and stir-fries.

Beans, Cannellini When I have the time, I love to make soup from scratch with dried navy or Great Northern beans. However, when I'm in a hurry, I've come to appreciate the convenience of canned white cannellini beans. They're great for soups, salads, and appetizers.

Biscuits, Rolls, and Pizza Crust Unbaked biscuits and rolls from the dairy case are wonderful for quick mini-pizzas. Unbaked pizza crusts are the next best thing to homemade dough. They also work well for calzone crust.

Bread Crumbs, Seasoned These make an easy topping for casseroles or vegetable dishes.

Broth While homemade stock is delicious, canned chicken and beef broth are reasonable substitutes. Most grocery stores sell $14\frac{1}{2}$-ounce cans of both beef and chicken broth. Some also carry 46-ounce cans and the new easy-to-pour 32-ounce cartons of chicken broth. Both regular chicken broth and reduced-sodium broth (which is also reduced in fat) are generally available.

Cheese, Cream You may not think of this as a convenience food, but when you combine it with milk and melt it over low heat in a saucepan, you have the basis for a quick cream-style pasta sauce. Incidentally, to lower the fat in many dishes, I generally use reduced-fat cream cheese or Neufchâtel. It has a third less fat than regular cream cheese and a very rich flavor.

Cheese, Mozzarella, Shredded For convenience, buy your mozzarella already shredded, and simply pour it from the bag into a measuring cup. I use part-skimmed mozzarella to cut down on the fat in many recipes.

Cheese, Parmesan, Grated The rich flavor of grated Parmesan will quickly enliven a whole range of Italian dishes—from creamy sauces to calzone filling and skillet entrees.

Chicken Breast, Boneless, Skinless, is a wonderful timesaver. All you have to do is cut it up and add it to a skillet dish or sauce.

Cookie Dough from the dairy case makes a wonderful crust for the Fruit Pizza on page 147.

Egg Substitute, Liquid, will save you time in baking recipes since you can pour and use it right from the carton. One-fourth cup of egg substitute equals one egg.

Espresso, Instant, means you don't have to crank up the espresso machine in order to make the easy Tiramisu on page 148.

Frozen Mixed Vegetable Combinations, particularly stir-fry peppers and onions, quickly add texture and variety to many dishes from appetizers and soups to main dishes. As an added bonus, the quality of these premium vegetable mixtures is often better than with regular frozen vegetables.

Garlic, Chopped You'll find small jars of already chopped garlic in the refrigerated produce section of most grocery stores. In large warehouse stores, you can buy much larger jars, which will keep in the refrigerator for several months.

Herbs, Fresh. Once an exotic ingredient, fresh herbs were previously available only to home gardeners and restaurants. Now they're sold in the produce section of most supermarkets and in many specialty shops. If you haven't tried fresh basil, for example, you'll be surprised by the difference it can make in a salad or in a simple recipe such as the Oven-Crisped Bread with Tomato and Basil.

Italian Dressing I've provided a recipe for a very good Italian dressing that you can use in a number of the salads in *Simply Italian*. It's easy and quick to make, but if you don't have the time for homemade dressing, your best alternative is a dry-mix dressing that comes with the spices in a packet. All you do is add oil, vinegar, and water. Or you may use any bottled Italian dressing you like. In some recipes, you may actually use less bottled dressing because the flavor is more intense.

Italian Seasoning Instead of measuring out individual quantities of thyme, oregano, basil, and rosemary, in many recipes I use a dried Italian seasoning mix sold in the spice department of most supermarkets.

Ladyfingers are perfect for the cake layer in elegant desserts like Tiramisu and Zuppa Inglese. Simply take them out of the package and sandwich them between layers of filling.

Lemon Juice Although bottled reconstituted lemon juice has a flavor I don't much like, there's a frozen variety that tastes almost as good as fresh. Thawed, it will keep in the refrigerator for several months.

Mashed Potatoes, Instant These make a wonderful and very convenient thickener for soups such as the Creamy Mushroom-Basil Soup on page 27.

Olives Not too long ago, buying high-quality olives meant a trip to an Italian deli. Now you can find them in the deli department at many supermarkets. While canned olives work well in many recipes, deli olives will give dishes such as the Marinated Artichokes, Olives, and Sun-Dried Tomatoes appetizer a distinctively authentic flavor.

Pasta, Fresh, is available in the dairy department of many supermarkets. Not only does it cook more quickly than dried pasta, but there's more variety such as stuffed shells, tortellini, and ravioli. If you want to buy similar products in larger quantities and store them for longer periods, purchase them from the frozen food section.

Pizza Sauce These thick, seasoned sauces are designed especially as pizza toppings.

Pizza Shells I've provided a quick pizza crust recipe in the Pizza chapter. If you don't have time to make your own, you can pick up one from the dairy case, the frozen food section, or the bread department of your supermarket.

Seasoned Tomato Sauces and Chopped Tomatoes On the market today are a number of already flavored tomato sauces and chopped tomatoes that are great for skillet dinners, soups, one-pot meals, and other dishes. Often they can be used with no other seasonings. I've called for Italian-seasoned sauce and tomatoes. But you can add variety to your cooking by trying some of the other flavors.

Spaghetti Sauces There are so many gourmet sauces available today that you can choose from a wide variety. Tomato-basil, roasted red pepper, mushroom. They'll each give you an Italian dinner with almost no preparation time.

Spinach, Frozen Leaf. Sold in a plastic bag, frozen leaf spinach is easy to use and easy to store since the leaves do not stick together like the old-style blocks of frozen spinach. You can take out just the amount you need for soups, dips, or other recipes.

Stuffing Mix Seasoned stuffing mix works well in many recipes that call for stale bread cubes—such as Stuffed Artichoke Casserole.

Tomato Paste is great for flavoring and thickening sauces and dressings. If you'll only be using a tablespoon or two, buy it in a tube. You can squeeze out a little and keep the rest in the refrigerator.

Turkey Cutlets are not really "cutlets." They're thin slices of turkey breast that cook in just a few minutes—which makes them perfect for dishes like the Turkey Cacciatore.

Vegetables, Fresh To save preparation time, for a small premium buy fresh vegetables such as mushrooms, celery, carrots, and onions already cut up from the salad bar. Or purchase baby carrots, which can go right into most dishes without cutting.

Vinegars and Oils, Flavored These give extra zip to salad dressing, marinades, and other dishes. A variety of flavorings is available—from mixed herb or basil to garlic and red pepper.

antipasti

Hot Artichoke Spread

Roasted Summer Vegetable Spread

Broiled Portobello Mushrooms

Pizza Puffs

Oven-Crisped Bread with Tomato and Basil

Tomato and Olive Spread

Sun-Dried Tomato and Peppers Spread

Marinated Artichokes, Olives, and Sun-Dried Tomatoes

Shrimp and Artichokes Vinaigrette

a n t i p a s t i

HOT ARTICHOKE SPREAD

A subtle blend of taste and texture, this artichoke spread is wonderfully rich and creamy. Serve on toasted Italian bread or crackers.

1	14–15-ounce can water-packed artichoke heart quarters, drained
1/3	cup grated Parmesan cheese
2/3	cup reduced-fat sour cream
1/4	cup Neufchâtel cream cheese, at room temperature
1/2	teaspoon chopped garlic
3–4	drops hot pepper sauce
1/4	cup chopped chives, *or* thinly sliced green onion tops

Remove and discard any tough outer leaves from artichoke hearts. Coarsely chop hearts. Set aside in a small bowl.

In a medium-sized bowl, combine Parmesan cheese, sour cream, Neufchâtel cheese, garlic, and hot pepper sauce. Stir with a spoon until well blended. Stir in artichoke hearts and chives. Transfer to a small glass or ceramic microwave-safe, ovenproof casserole or bowl. Cover with casserole lid or wax paper, and microwave on High power about 3 to 4 minutes or until heated through. Serve hot.

HELPFUL HINT:

You can keep this spread warm on a hot tray. Or simply return it to the microwave for a minute or two when it begins to cool down.

PREPARATION TIME:

12 minutes

COOKING TIME:

3 minutes

SERVINGS: *32*

PER SERVING:
Calories: 18
Protein (g): 1.1
Carbohydrates (g): 1.2
Fat (g): 0.9
Saturated Fat (g): 0.6
Cholesterol (mg): 3
Dietary Fiber (g): 0
Sodium (mg): 53

ROASTED SUMMER VEGETABLE SPREAD

Roasting does wonders for these simple vegetables. Serve warm on small slices of Italian bread or crackers.

PREPARATION TIME:
12 minutes
COOKING TIME:
45 minutes
SERVINGS: *24*
1 tablespoon each
(1 1/2 cups)

6 plum tomatoes, chopped
1 cup diced zucchini
1 cup very thinly sliced onion
1 red bell pepper, seeded and chopped
1 tablespoon olive oil
1/4 teaspoon chopped garlic
1/4 teaspoon dried basil leaves
   Salt and pepper to taste

Preheat oven to 400 degrees.

Spray a 9- by 13-inch baking pan with non-stick spray and set aside. In pan, combine tomatoes, zucchini, onion, pepper, oil, garlic, and basil. Sprinkle with salt and pepper, if desired.

Toss to mix. Bake in the center of the oven for 40 to 45 minutes, stirring occasionally, or until onion is tender.

Serve warm on toasted Italian bread slices or crackers (not included in nutritional data).

PER SERVING:
Calories: 16
Protein (g): 0.4
Carbohydrates (g): 2.4
Fat (g): 0.7
Saturated Fat (g): 0.1
Cholesterol (mg): 0
Dietary Fiber (g): 0.6
Sodium (mg): 3

BROILED PORTOBELLO MUSHROOMS

These mushrooms are wonderfully rich-tasting and satisfying and at the same time easy to make and relatively lean.

4	large portobello mushrooms (about 1¼ pounds total), stems removed
2	tablespoons extra-virgin olive oil
1½	tablespoons lemon juice
¼	cup thin 1-inch-long strips red bell pepper
¾	teaspoon dried thyme leaves
⅛	teaspoon (generous) pepper
½	teaspoon salt, *or more to taste*
1	teaspoon minced garlic
	Escarole, *or* endive, leaves for garnish
1–2	tablespoons finely chopped fresh chives, *or* green onions

Preheat broiler to very hot, using highest setting. Adjust oven rack to about 4 inches from broiler element.

Lightly rub smooth side of mushroom caps with a little olive oil. Arrange mushroom caps, gill side up, on a broiler pan or small heavy-duty rimmed baking sheet.

In a small bowl, stir together oil, lemon juice, pepper strips, thyme, pepper, salt, and garlic until well blended. Sprinkle mixture over mushrooms, dividing it equally among them. Let marinate for 8 to 10 minutes.

Broil mushrooms 5 or 6 minutes until just cooked through. Working on a cutting board, slice the caps crosswise on a diagonal into thick slices.

To serve immediately, arrange slices on small plates on escarole leaves. Spoon some pan juices and cooked pepper strips over the slices. Sprinkle chives over mushrooms, dividing it equally among them.

HELPFUL HINT:

For convenience, this dish can be made ahead and reheated. Refrigerate the cooked mushroom caps and any juice for up to 24 hours. Then slice caps and reheat in a microwave oven until hot. Serve as directed above.

PREPARATION AND MARINATION TIME:
15 minutes
COOKING TIME:
6 minutes
SERVINGS: **4**

PER SERVING:
Calories: 104
Protein (g): 4.8
Carbohydrates (g): 5.2
Fat (g): 9.4
Saturated Fat (g): 1.3
Cholesterol (mg): 0
Dietary Fiber (g): 1.3
Sodium (mg): 297

PIZZA PUFFS

These puffy little pizzas make a great snack or appetizer.

PREPARATION TIME:

8 minutes

COOKING TIME:

8 minutes

SERVINGS: *10*

1	7.5-ounce package unbaked refrigerator biscuits, *or* rolls
3	tablespoons seasoned tomato sauce, pizza sauce, *or* spaghetti sauce
$\frac{1}{4}$	cup reduced-fat shredded mozzarella cheese
2–3	tablespoons chopped black, *or* green, olives (optional)

Preheat oven to 450 degrees. Spray a small baking sheet with non-stick spray. Set aside.

Open carton and separate biscuits. Place on baking sheet.

With a small spoon, spread tomato sauce on biscuits, dividing mixture evenly. Top with the cheese, dividing evenly. Top with chopped olives, if desired, dividing evenly. Bake in center of oven for 8 to 10 minutes or until golden. Serve hot.

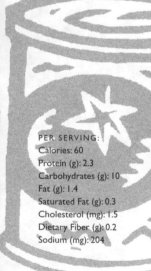

PER SERVING:
Calories: 60
Protein (g): 2.3
Carbohydrates (g): 10
Fat (g): 1.4
Saturated Fat (g): 0.3
Cholesterol (mg): 1.5
Dietary Fiber (g): 0.2
Sodium (mg): 204

OVEN-CRISPED BREAD WITH TOMATO AND BASIL

In Italy I learned to love toasted Italian bread appetizers, although I always wished the fat content weren't quite so high. Here's a slightly lower-fat rendition that retains the great garlic and Parmesan taste.

PREPARATION TIME:

5 minutes

COOKING TIME:

10 minutes

SERVINGS: **12–13**

1	13-ounce loaf unsliced Italian bread
2	tablespoons olive oil
1½	tablespoons chicken, *or* vegetable, broth
1½	tablespoons red wine vinegar
1	teaspoon minced garlic
1	teaspoon dried basil leaves
⅓	cup grated Parmesan cheese
2	medium-sized tomatoes, cut into ¼-inch slices
	Salt to taste
12	fresh basil leaves

Preheat oven to 375 degrees.

Discard heels of bread. Cut remainder of bread into ¾-inch slices. Arrange bread on a large rimmed baking sheet. Set aside.

In a 2-cup measure, combine oil, broth, vinegar, garlic, and basil. Stir to mix well.

With a pastry brush, spread mixture evenly over bread slices. Sprinkle evenly with Parmesan cheese. Bake in preheated oven for 10 to 15 minutes until bread begins to brown. Top each bread slice with a tomato slice. Sprinkle lightly with salt, if desired. Add a basil leaf to each. Serve immediately.

HELPFUL HINT:

A pastry brush makes spreading the oil mixture on the bread very easy. (For easy clean up, put the brush in the dishwasher.) If you don't have a pastry brush, you can spoon the oil mixture over the bread slices and spread it with your finger or the back of the spoon.

PER SERVING:
Calories: 109
Protein (g): 3.6
Carbohydrates (g): 15.3
Fat (g): 3.8
Saturated Fat (g): 0.9
Cholesterol (mg): 1.6
Dietary Fiber (g): 1
Sodium (mg): 213

TOMATO AND OLIVE SPREAD

In summer, when you can get vine-ripened tomatoes, use them in this tasty spread. In winter, use plum tomatoes. Serve on toasted Italian bread or crackers.

PREPARATION TIME:

12 minutes

SERVINGS: *48*

2	medium tomatoes, coarsely chopped
25	large ripe pitted olives, sliced
1/2	teaspoon chopped garlic
1	tablespoon olive oil
1	teaspoon balsamic vinegar
	Salt and pepper to taste

In a medium bowl, combine tomatoes, olives, garlic, oil, and vinegar. Transfer to a food processor container, and process with 4 or 5 on-off bursts to blend the vegetables. Do not overchop. Add salt and pepper to taste, if desired.

Serve immediately on small slices of toasted Italian bread or crackers (not included in nutritional data). Or cover and refrigerate several hours. Drain off excess liquid and stir before serving. Leftovers will keep in the refrigerator 3 or 4 days.

PER SERVING:
Calories: 6
Protein (g): 0.1
Carbohydrates (g): 0.4
Fat (g): 0.5
Saturated Fat (g): 0.1
Cholesterol (mg): 0
Dietary Fiber (g): 0.1
Sodium (mg): 20

SUN-DRIED TOMATO AND PEPPERS SPREAD

Here, simple ingredients produce a rich and flavorful spread. The secret is in cooking the vegetable mixture until the peppers are very tender. Serve on toasted Italian bread or crackers.

PREPARATION TIME:

12 minutes

COOKING TIME:

10 minutes

SERVINGS: **24**

3/4 cup dry-packed sun-dried tomatoes
1 16-ounce bag mixed frozen peppers and onion stir-fry
1 tablespoon olive oil
1 teaspoon minced garlic
2 teaspoons Italian seasoning
Salt and pepper to taste
1/2 cup reduced-fat grated mozzarella cheese

In a small bowl, cover tomatoes with hot water. Let sit for 5 to 10 minutes to soften. Drain and chop. Cut up any large pieces of onion in peppers-onion mixture.

In a 12-inch non-stick skillet, combine reserved tomatoes, peppers and onion mixture, oil, garlic, Italian seasoning, and salt and black pepper, if desired. Stir to mix well.

Cook uncovered over medium heat 10 to 15 minutes, stirring frequently, until onions and peppers are tender. Remove from heat. Transfer to a shallow bowl. Stir in cheese.

Serve warm with Italian bread or non-fat crackers (not included in nutritional data).

HELPFUL HINT:

Keep this spread warm on a hot tray, or microwave it for 1 or 2 minutes when it begins to cool.

PER SERVING:
Calories: 23
Protein (g): 1.2
Carbohydrates (g): 2.3
Fat (g): 1
Saturated Fat (g): 0.3
Cholesterol (mg): 1.3
Dietary Fiber (g): 0.7
Sodium (mg): 57

MARINATED ARTICHOKES, OLIVES, AND SUN-DRIED TOMATOES

You might find this easy appetizer served at a little inn in a northern Italian hill town. The recipe calls for imported oil-cured olives, which are available at many large grocery stores or Italian specialty markets.

PREPARATION TIME:

6 minutes

COOKING TIME:

2 minutes

SERVINGS:

72, 1 tablespoon each

$1/2$ cup dry-packed sun-dried tomatoes

2 14–15-ounce cans water-packed artichoke heart quarters, drained

1 cup oil-cured olives

$1/2$ cup homemade, *or* commercial, Italian Dressing (see page 15)

$1/4$ cup thinly sliced green onion tops

Place tomatoes and $1/4$ cup water in a 1-cup measure. Cover with wax paper, and microwave 2 minutes on High power to soften. Drain. Cool in a colander under cold running water. When tomatoes are cool enough to handle, cut in half.

Remove and discard any tough outer leaves from artichoke hearts.

In a medium bowl, combine tomatoes, artichoke hearts, olives, dressing, and onions. Stir to mix well.

Cover and refrigerate 3 hours or up to 24 hours before serving. Serve with toothpicks.

HELPFUL HINT:

You can use either Italian olives for this recipe or Greek kalamata olives. If you like, you can substitute green pimiento-stuffed olives.

PER SERVING:

Calories: 12
Protein (g): 0.4
Carbohydrates (g): 1.1
Fat (g): 0.7
Saturated Fat (g): 0.1
Cholesterol (mg): 0
Dietary Fiber (g): 0.1
Sodium (mg): 106

SHRIMP AND ARTICHOKES VINAIGRETTE

Although I've put this tasty shrimp and artichoke mixture in the appetizer section, you can also serve it as a salad on lettuce or other greens. If you like, substitute a commercial dressing for the homemade.

1 recipe Italian Dressing (see page 15)
¼ teaspoon dry mustard
1 14–15-ounce can water-packed artichoke heart quarters, drained
12 ounces cooked and ready-to-eat medium shrimp
2 tablespoons thinly sliced green onion tops

Add mustard to Italian Dressing and stir or shake to mix well. Set aside.

Remove any coarse outer leaves from artichoke hearts. Combine artichoke hearts, shrimp, and green onion in a medium bowl. Stir in dressing mixture. Cover and refrigerate at least 1 hour and up to 24 hours, stirring occasionally. Before serving, drain off most of the dressing mixture. Serve with toothpicks.

PREPARATION TIME:

10 minutes

SERVINGS: **20**

PER SERVING:
Calories: 73
Protein (g): 4.1
Carbohydrates (g): 1.6
Fat (g): 5.6
Saturated Fat (g): 0.8
Cholesterol (mg): 33.2
Dietary Fiber (g): 0
Sodium (mg): 146

salads

Italian Dressing

Caesar Salad

Bread Salad

Binnie's Pasta Salad

Ravioli Salad

Rice Salad

Italian Garden Orzo Salad

Tuna-Pasta Salad

ITALIAN DRESSING

The fresh taste of homemade salad dressing is so superior to the bottled variety that you'll want to make it frequently. This dressing tastes great on green salads. I also use it in a number of recipes throughout the book.

$^1\!/_2$ cup olive oil

2 tablespoons lemon juice

2 tablespoons red wine, *or* cider, vinegar

2 tablespoons water

$^1\!/_2$ teaspoon chopped garlic

$^1\!/_2$ teaspoon *each* salt and sugar

$^1\!/_2$ teaspoon dried thyme leaves

$^1\!/_4$ teaspoon *each* dry mustard and dried oregano leaves

$^1\!/_8$ teaspoon white pepper

Combine all ingredients in a small jar with a tight-fitting lid. Shake to mix. The dressing will keep in the refrigerator for about 2 weeks.

PREPARATION TIME:

8 minutes

SERVINGS:

14, 1 tablespoon each (makes $^7\!/_8$ cup)

PER SERVING:
Calories: 70
Protein (g): 0
Carbohydrates (g): 0.4
Fat (g): 7.7
Saturated Fat (g): 1
Cholesterol (mg): 0
Dietary Fiber (g): 0.1
Sodium (mg): 83

CAESAR SALAD

You don't have to wait for a night out at an Italian restaurant to enjoy Caesar Salad. Here's a quick and easy recipe to make at home.

PREPARATION TIME:
15 minutes
SERVINGS: **6**

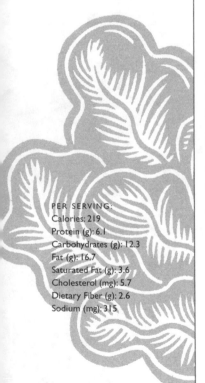

$^1/_3$ cup olive oil
  2 tablespoons water
  2 tablespoons lemon juice
$^1/_2$ cup grated Parmesan cheese, divided
  2 teaspoons Worcestershire sauce
  1 teaspoon minced garlic
     Salt and pepper to taste
12 cups romaine lettuce, washed, dried, and torn into bite-size pieces
  2 cups Caesar-style croutons

In a medium-sized jar with a tight-fitting lid, combine oil, water, lemon juice, 3 tablespoons of the Parmesan, Worcestershire sauce, garlic, and salt and pepper, if desired. Shake to mix well. Set aside.

Place lettuce pieces in a large serving bowl.

Add croutons to the salad bowl. Toss lettuce and croutons with remaining Parmesan cheese.

Add the dressing to the bowl, and toss to mix well.

PER SERVING:
Calories: 219
Protein (g): 6.1
Carbohydrates (g): 12.3
Fat (g): 16.7
Saturated Fat (g): 3.6
Cholesterol (mg): 5.7
Dietary Fiber (g): 2.6
Sodium (mg): 315

BREAD SALAD

I was introduced to this salad at one of New York's most exclusive Italian restaurants and loved the concept, since the crunchy cubes make such a nice contrast to the crisp greens. To keep the bread crisp, be sure to dry the romaine well after rinsing it.

DRESSING:

    3 tablespoons olive oil
    2 tablespoons Parmesan cheese
    1 tablespoon red wine vinegar
    1 tablespoon water
      Salt and pepper to taste

SALAD:

    7–8 large romaine lettuce leaves, torn into pieces (about 6 cups)
    2 large tomatoes, cubed
    1 medium cucumber, peeled, seeded, and cubed
    ¼ cup thinly sliced chives, *or* green onion tops
    ¼ cup chopped fresh basil leaves, *or* 1 teaspoon dried basil leaves
    2 cups Caesar-style croutons

In a 2-cup measure or similar deep bowl, whisk together oil, Parmesan, vinegar, water, and salt and pepper, if desired. Set aside.

Rinse the romaine, and dry well with paper towels or tea towel. In a large salad bowl, mix together romaine, tomato, cucumber, chives, and fresh basil. (If using dried basil, mix it into the salad dressing.)

Pour the dressing over all, and toss to mix. Lightly toss in the croutons. Serve at once.

Alternatively, to prepare salad 6 to 8 hours ahead, make dressing and refrigerate. Prepare salad ingredients, and transfer to serving bowl. Just before serving, assemble salad.

PREPARATION TIME:
15 minutes
SERVINGS: **6–8**

PER SERVING:
Calories: 116
Protein (g): 2.9
Carbohydrates (g): 10
Fat (g): 7.5
Saturated Fat (g): 1.5
Cholesterol (mg): 1.3
Dietary Fiber (g): 1.9
Sodium (mg): 154

BINNIE'S PASTA SALAD

"Tangy" is the right description for this pasta salad, which is adapted from a recipe given to me by a very dear friend. If summer tomatoes are unavailable, substitute 5 or 6 Italian plum tomatoes.

PREPARATION TIME:

20 minutes

COOKING TIME:

12 minutes

SERVINGS: **7–8**

1 1/4 cups uncooked elbow macaroni

1 recipe Italian Dressing (page 15)

2 tablespoons tomato paste

1/4 teaspoon dry mustard

1 large tomato, cubed

1/4 cup chopped chives, *or* sliced green onion tops

1 large red bell pepper, seeded and chopped

2 cups broccoli florets

Cook macaroni according to package directions. Transfer to a colander, and rinse under cold running water. Drain.

Meanwhile, in a large bowl, combine Italian Dressing with tomato paste and mustard. Stir to mix well. Add tomato, chives, bell pepper, and broccoli.

Stir to mix well. Stir in macaroni. Refrigerate one hour or up to 36 hours before serving. Stir before serving.

PER SERVING:
Calories: 199
Protein (g): 3.2
Carbohydrates (g): 16.4
Fat (g): 14
Saturated Fat (g): 1.9
Cholesterol (mg): 0
Dietary Fiber (g): 1.7
Sodium (mg): 187

RAVIOLI SALAD

For a change of pace, try this hearty main-dish salad. If you like, you can make it the day before it's needed.

1 9-ounce package dairy case cheese ravioli, *or* 2 cups frozen ravioli
1 recipe Italian Dressing (page 15), *or* $^3/_4$ cup commercial Italian dressing
1 medium tomato, cubed
$^1/_4$ cup chopped chives, *or* sliced green onion tops
1 large red bell pepper, seeded and chopped
2 cups small broccoli, *or* cauliflower, florets
$^1/_2$ cup sliced oil-cured olives, *or* regular canned black olives

Cook ravioli according to package directions. Transfer to a colander and rinse under cold running water. Drain.

Meanwhile, in a large bowl, combine dressing with tomato, chives, bell pepper, broccoli, and olives.

Stir to mix well. Stir in ravioli. Serve at room temperature. Or refrigerate several hours before serving. Stir before serving.

HELPFUL HINT:

If you don't want to use homemade dressing, the closest equivalent is the type that comes in a dry packet that you mix with oil, vinegar, and water.

PREPARATION TIME:
10 minutes
COOKING TIME:
5 minutes
SERVINGS: **6**

PER SERVING:
Calories: 354
Protein (g): 7.9
Carbohydrates (g): 20.5
Fat (g): 28.2
Saturated Fat (g): 5.8
Cholesterol (mg): 15.2
Dietary Fiber (g): 2.5
Sodium (mg): 745

RICE SALAD

This hearty salad comes from a wonderful little restaurant in the Italian hill town of San Gimignano. Although it was served as an accompaniment to our main dish, I like to showcase it as a lunch or summer supper entree.

PREPARATION TIME:

12 minutes

COOKING TIME:

22 minutes

SERVINGS: *6, side dish*

1 cup long-grain white rice
1 large red, *or* yellow, bell pepper, seeded and cubed
1 cup shredded cabbage
¼ cup minced chives, *or* thinly sliced green onion tops
18–20 pitted black olives, sliced
4 ounces turkey, *or* beef, sausage, diced
½ cup homemade Italian Dressing (page 15), *or* commercial dressing

Cook rice according to package directions.

In a large serving bowl, combine bell pepper, cabbage, chives, and olives. Set aside.

While rice is cooking, in a medium-sized non-stick skillet, cook sausage over medium heat until it is heated through and begins to brown, 2 or 3 minutes. Stir sausage into vegetable mixture. Stir in dressing.

When rice is cooked, add to bowl, and stir to mix well. Serve warm, or cover and refrigerate several hours. Stir before serving.

HELPFUL HINT:

If you like, the salad can be made the day before needed and refrigerated.

PER SERVING:
Calories: 270
Protein (g): 5.8
Carbohydrates (g): 28
Fat (g): 15.3
Saturated Fat (g): 2.1
Cholesterol (mg): 14.9
Dietary Fiber (g): 1
Sodium (mg): 341

ITALIAN GARDEN ORZO SALAD

Colorful, fresh tasting, and easy, this makes a nice addition to a buffet or picnic. It needs to chill at least 30 minutes before serving and can be prepared a day ahead, if desired.

1 1/4 cups (about 8 ounces) uncooked orzo
1 cup *each* diced carrots and celery
1 cup *each* diced red and yellow bell peppers
1/4 cup chopped green onions, *or* finely chopped fresh chives
1/3 cup fresh lemon juice
1/2 cup chopped fresh parsley leaves
3 tablespoons extra-virgin olive oil
1/2 teaspoon dried marjoram leaves
1/2 teaspoon finely grated lemon zest (yellow part of peel)
1/4 teaspoon *each* salt and pepper, plus more to taste
Romaine, *or* other crisp, lettuce leaves for garnish

Cook orzo according to package directions until just *al dente*. Turn out into a colander. Rinse under cold water; drain well.

In a large serving bowl, stir together carrots, celery, bell peppers, and green onions.

In a small non-reactive bowl, mix lemon juice, parsley, oil, marjoram, lemon zest, and salt, and pepper until well blended. Pour mixture over diced vegetables. Add orzo, tossing until thoroughly blended. Add more salt and pepper, if desired.

Refrigerate at least 30 minutes and up to 24 hours, if desired. Serve on lettuce leaves, if desired.

PREPARATION TIME:
18 minutes
COOKING AND CHILLING
TIME:
38 minutes
SERVINGS: **7**

PER SERVING:
Calories: 196
Protein (g): 4.9
Carbohydrates (g): 30.1
Fat (g): 6.5
Saturated Fat (g): 0.9
Cholesterol (mg): 0
Dietary Fiber (g): 2.6
Sodium (mg): 108

TUNA-PASTA SALAD

For a tangy change from traditional American tuna salad, try this version with artichoke hearts, black olives, and pasta. Use either the Italian Dressing on page 15 or a purchased dressing.

PREPARATION TIME:

15 minutes

COOKING TIME:

12 minutes

SERVINGS: **6**

1½ cups penne pasta, cooked according to package directions
1 14–15-ounce can water-packed artichoke heart quarters, drained
4 Italian plum tomatoes, cut into bite-size pieces
1 cup cubed zucchini
¼ cup thinly sliced green onion tops
¼ cup sliced pitted black olives
½ cup homemade Italian Dressing (page 15), *or* commercial dressing
1 6-ounce can water-packed solid white tuna, drained and flaked

Cool the pasta under cold running water; drain.

Pull off and discard any tough outer leaves from artichoke hearts. In a large bowl, combine artichoke hearts, pasta, tomatoes, zucchini, onions, and olives. Stir to mix well. Stir in dressing. Fold in tuna. Serve at room temperature, or refrigerate several hours or up to 24 hours before serving.

HELPFUL HINT:

Although the recipe calls for plum tomatoes, in summer you can use two medium vine-ripened tomatoes.

PER SERVING:
Calories: 288
Protein (g): 13.4
Carbohydrates (g): 29.4
Fat (g): 13.3
Saturated Fat (g): 1.8
Cholesterol (mg): 8.5
Dietary Fiber (g): 1.9
Sodium (mg): 567

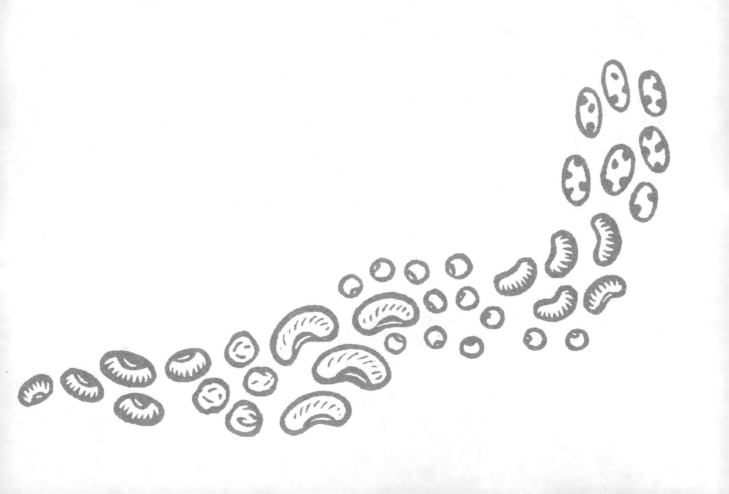

soups

Creamy Mushroom-Basil Soup

Hearty Minestrone with Pepperoni

Chick-Pea and Pasta Minestrone

Bean and Spinach Soup

Potato and Onion Soup

Lentil-Vegetable Soup

Easy Italian Fish Soup

Pasta Soup with Greens

s o u p s

CREAMY MUSHROOM-BASIL SOUP

This wonderful creamy soup takes only minutes to make, because it's thickened with instant mashed potatoes. In summer I love to make it with fresh basil. But dried works well, too.

- 1 tablespoon butter *or* margarine
- 4 cups reduced-sodium, *or* regular, chicken broth, divided
- 8 ounces fresh mushrooms, sliced
- 1 teaspoon chopped garlic
- ½ cup whole milk
- 2 tablespoons dry sherry
- ¼ cup chopped fresh basil *or* 2 teaspoons dried basil leaves
    Salt and white pepper to taste
- 1¼ cups instant mashed potatoes

In a large Dutch oven or similar large, heavy pot, melt butter. Add 3 tablespoons of broth, mushrooms, and garlic; and cook, stirring, over medium-high heat, about 3 or 4 minutes, until the mushrooms are partially cooked. Add remaining broth, milk, sherry, basil, and salt and pepper, if desired. Stir in mashed potatoes. Bring to boil. Reduce heat, and simmer, stirring occasionally, an additional 10 minutes to allow flavors to blend.

PREPARATION TIME:
6 minutes
COOKING TIME:
14 minutes
SERVINGS: 4

PER SERVING:
Calories: 177
Protein (g): 6.4
Carbohydrates (g): 21.3
Fat (g): 7.1
Saturated Fat (g): 3.7
Cholesterol (mg): 12.5
Dietary Fiber (g): 2.4
Sodium (mg): 112

HEARTY MINESTRONE WITH PEPPERONI

Pepperoni is quite flavorful so a little goes a long way in this full-bodied soup. Serve along with crusty bread and a salad for an easy, satisfying supper.

PREPARATION TIME:
17 minutes

COOKING TIME:
35 minutes

SERVINGS: **6**

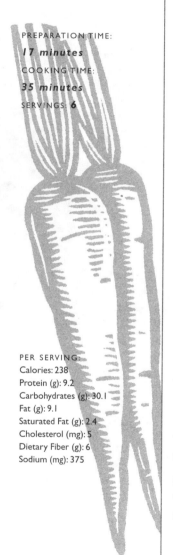

1½ tablespoons olive oil, preferably extra-virgin
1 large onion, chopped
2 large celery stalks, coarsely diced
2 medium-sized carrots, coarsely diced
1½ teaspoons minced garlic
⅓ cup finely diced pepperoni, *or* hard salami
5½ cups reduced-sodium, *or* regular, chicken broth
1 large boiling potato, peeled and diced
2 teaspoons *each* dried basil leaves and dried marjoram leaves
½ cup uncooked small macaroni
1 medium zucchini, diced
1 19-ounce can cannellini beans, rinsed and well drained
  Salt and pepper to taste

PER SERVING:
Calories: 238
Protein (g): 9.2
Carbohydrates (g): 30.1
Fat (g): 9.1
Saturated Fat (g): 2.4
Cholesterol (mg): 5
Dietary Fiber (g): 6
Sodium (mg): 375

In a 4-quart Dutch oven or similar large, heavy pot, heat oil to hot, but not smoking, over high heat. Add onion, celery, and carrots. Cook, stirring, about 5 minutes until vegetables begin to brown. Add garlic and pepperoni; cook 2 minutes longer.

Add broth, potato, basil, and marjoram. Bring mixture to a boil, stirring occasionally. Lower heat; simmer, covered, for 15 minutes.

Bring mixture to a rolling boil. Stir in macaroni and zucchini. When mixture returns to a boil, adjust heat so it boils gently. Cook 8 to 10 minutes or until macaroni is almost tender.

Stir in beans. Simmer 4 to 5 minutes longer until vegetables are tender and flavors are well blended. If necessary, thin soup to desired consistency with water or broth. Add salt and pepper, if desired.

CHICK-PEA AND PASTA MINESTRONE

Try this interesting minestrone variation. Substantial and wonderfully flavorful, it's a snap to make. If you don't have the leftover ham, you can use a ham slice.

PREPARATION TIME:

12 minutes

COOKING TIME:

30 minutes

SERVINGS: *7–8*

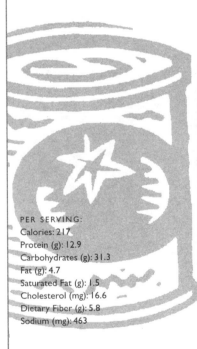

1	large onion, chopped
1	1-pound bag frozen mixed broccoli, carrots, and cauliflower
2	cups thinly sliced cabbage
1½	teaspoons chopped garlic
6	cups reduced-sodium, *or regular*, chicken broth
1	15-ounce can chick-peas, rinsed and drained
1	15-ounce can reduced-sodium, *or regular*, tomato sauce
2	teaspoons Italian seasoning
8	ounces leftover reduced-sodium ham, cut into small pieces (1½ cups)
1	large pork hock
¼	teaspoon black pepper
½	cup (3 ounces) uncooked orzo

In a Dutch oven or similar heavy pot, combine all ingredients. Cover and simmer 30 to 35 minutes, stirring occasionally until flavors are well blended.

Remove and discard pork hock. With a large, shallow spoon, skim and discard any fat from top of soup.

PER SERVING:
Calories: 217
Protein (g): 12.9
Carbohydrates (g): 31.3
Fat (g): 4.7
Saturated Fat (g): 1.5
Cholesterol (mg): 16.6
Dietary Fiber (g): 5.8
Sodium (mg): 463

BEAN AND SPINACH SOUP

Beans and spinach are a classic Italian combination—which I've used together in this hearty soup.

PREPARATION TIME:
8 minutes

COOKING TIME:

26 minutes

SERVINGS: **5–6, main dish**

6 cups reduced-sodium, *or* regular, chicken broth

1/2 cup uncooked orzo

6 ounces Canadian bacon, cut into thin slivers

1 tablespoon Italian seasoning

1/2 teaspoon minced garlic

1/8 teaspoon black pepper

1 15-ounce can reduced-sodium, *or* regular, tomato sauce

1 19-ounce can cannellini beans, undrained

2 cups loose-pack frozen spinach

Salt to taste

In a large, heavy pot, bring broth to a boil. Add orzo, bacon, Italian seasoning, garlic, and pepper. Cook, uncovered, 11 to 12 minutes or until orzo is tender. Add tomato sauce and beans. Return to a boil, reduce heat, and simmer, covered, an additional 12 minutes, stirring occasionally. Add spinach, bring to a boil again, and cook an additional 3 minutes. Add salt, if desired.

PER SERVING:
Calories: 236
Protein (g): 16
Carbohydrates (g): 31.1
Fat (g): 5.4
Saturated Fat (g): 1.7
Cholesterol (mg): 13.5
Dietary Fiber (g): 6.9
Sodium (mg): 657

POTATO AND ONION SOUP

This is a simple but delicious soup that would normally be served as a first course at an Italian meal. However, I love it as a luncheon entree or the centerpiece for a light supper.

3	cups chopped onions
2	teaspoons chopped garlic
1	tablespoon olive oil
1	tablespoon butter, *or* margarine
5	cups beef broth, divided
5	cups peeled and cubed ($^1/_2$ inch) boiling potatoes
1$^1/_2$	teaspoons Italian seasoning
	Salt and pepper to taste
	Grated Parmesan cheese for garnish

In a Dutch oven or similar large, heavy pot, combine onions, garlic, oil, butter, and 3 tablespoons of broth. Cook over medium-high heat, stirring frequently, until onions are softened and begin to brown, about 8 minutes.

Add remaining broth, potatoes, and Italian seasoning. Bring to a boil. Reduce heat, cover, and simmer 10 to 15 minutes or until potatoes are tender.

When potatoes are done, use a potato masher to break them up so that the liquid is thickened slightly. Add salt and pepper, if desired.

Sprinkle each serving generously with grated Parmesan cheese.

HELPFUL HINT:

If you're using thin-skinned potatoes, there's no need to peel them before cubing.

PREPARATION TIME:
16 minutes
COOKING TIME:
18 minutes
SERVINGS: *6*

PER SERVING:
Calories: 325
Protein (g): 7.4
Carbohydrates (g): 61.2
Fat (g): 6.2
Saturated Fat (g): 2
Cholesterol (mg): 7.5
Dietary Fiber (g): 4.6
Sodium (mg): 708

LENTIL-VEGETABLE SOUP

Brown lentils do take some simmering, but unlike many legumes they don't require pre-soaking or any attention during cooking. They lend a wonderful homey flavor and heartiness to this simple soup.

PREPARATION TIME:
12 minutes
COOKING TIME:
50 minutes
SERVINGS: *6*

1	tablespoon olive oil
1/2	cup *each* chopped onion, carrot, and celery
1/3	cup well-trimmed diced smoked ham
2/3	cup brown lentils
4	cups reduced-sodium, *or* regular, chicken broth
1/8–1/4	teaspoon dried hot red pepper flakes, *or* to taste
1	small (1/2-pound) smoked pork hock (optional)
1	14 1/2-ounce can stewed tomatoes (including juice), chopped
	Salt and pepper to taste

Combine oil, onion, carrot, celery, and ham in a large soup pot or Dutch oven over high heat. Cook, stirring, until onions begin to brown, about 4 minutes.

Stir in lentils, broth, pepper flakes, and pork hock, if desired. Bring to a simmer. Adjust heat so soup simmers, and cook 35 to 40 minutes or until lentils are tender. Add tomatoes, and salt and pepper, if desired. Simmer until flavors are blended, about 8 minutes longer. Discard pork hock and serve.

HELPFUL HINTS:

The pork hock isn't essential, but it makes for a richer, smokier-tasting soup. Since it takes a while for the heat of the dried hot red pepper to permeate the broth, unless you like your soup really spicy it's best to start with 1/8 teaspoon pepper flakes and add more at the end if desired.

PER SERVING:
Calories: 148
Protein (g): 9.3
Carbohydrates (g): 19.4
Fat (g): 4.5
Saturated Fat (g): 1.1
Cholesterol (mg): 3
Dietary Fiber (g): 7.9
Sodium (mg): 268

EASY ITALIAN FISH SOUP

It's surprising how such a simple combination of ingredients can yield such savory results. This makes a good, healthful hurry-up meal.

1½ tablespoons olive oil
½ teaspoon minced garlic
1 large onion, chopped
1 large celery stalk, chopped
1 14½-ounce can reduced-sodium, *or* regular, diced tomatoes, including juice
¼ cup dry white wine, *or* sherry
1 8-ounce bottle clam juice
¼ cup chopped fresh parsley leaves, plus 2 tablespoons for garnish
1 teaspoon dried marjoram leaves
1 pound fresh, *or* frozen, boneless, skinless halibut, red snapper, *or* other white-fleshed fish, cut into 1-inch chunks
Salt and pepper to taste

In a 4-quart pot or saucepan, heat oil to hot, but not smoking, over high heat. Add garlic, onion, and celery. Lower heat slightly, and cook, stirring, until vegetables are well browned, about 5 minutes.

Stir in tomatoes, wine, clam juice, ¼ cup parsley, and marjoram. Reduce heat so mixture simmers gently. Simmer, uncovered, for 20 minutes. Add fish and continue simmering 3 to 5 minutes longer until pieces are just cooked through. Add salt and pepper, if desired. Garnish with additional parsley.

HELPFUL HINT:

Although the results won't be quite the same, in a pinch you can substitute 1 cup chicken broth for the clam juice.

PREPARATION TIME:
12 minutes
COOKING TIME:
30 minutes
SERVINGS: *4, main dish*

PER SERVING:
Calories: 217
Protein (g): 25.3
Carbohydrates (g): 8.9
Fat (g): 7.9
Saturated Fat (g): 1.1
Cholesterol (mg): 36.1
Dietary Fiber (g): 2.1
Sodium (mg): 224

PASTA SOUP WITH GREENS

Both escarole and spinach yield tasty, though very different, results in this soup. Choose the escarole for a more robust taste, spinach for milder flavor. You can also use escarole and spinach in combination.

PREPARATION TIME:
17 minutes
COOKING TIME:
16 minutes
SERVINGS: **4**

1	medium leek, roots and 3 inches of top removed
1	tablespoon olive oil
1	small onion, chopped
4	cups reduced-sodium, *or* regular, chicken broth
1½	teaspoons dried marjoram leaves
¼	cup uncooked tiny soup pasta, such as acini de peppe (barley-shaped), *or* stellini (star-shaped)
1½	cups well-washed and drained chopped escarole, *or* spinach, leaves (coarse ribs or stems removed)
	Salt and pepper to taste
2–3	tablespoons grated Parmesan cheese for garnish (optional)

Peel off and discard tough outer leaves and dry top parts of leek. Slice leek lengthwise into quarters; then coarsely chop. Rinse well in a colander. Transfer leek to a large bowl of water. Swish back and forth to remove any grit trapped between layers. Let stand several minutes to allow grit to sink to bottom. Then lift out leek. Rinse in a colander again; drain well.

In a large pot or very large saucepan, heat oil to hot, but not smoking, over high heat. Add leek and onion. Lower heat slightly, and cook, stirring, until lightly browned, about 6 minutes.

Stir in broth, marjoram, pasta, and escarole. Bring to a boil over high heat. Reduce heat so mixture simmers gently. Simmer, uncovered, stirring occasionally, until pasta is cooked through, about 10 minutes. Thin the soup with a little more broth or water, if necessary. Add salt and pepper, if desired.

Serve sprinkled with Parmesan, if desired.

With tiny star-shaped or other soup pasta kept on hand, it's always possible to cook up a simple pasta soup quickly.

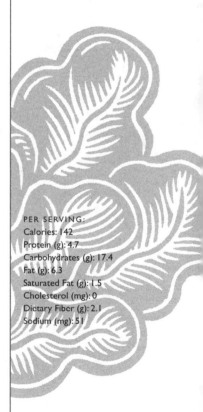

PER SERVING:
Calories: 142
Protein (g): 4.7
Carbohydrates (g): 17.4
Fat (g): 6.3
Saturated Fat (g): 1.5
Cholesterol (mg): 0
Dietary Fiber (g): 2.1
Sodium (mg): 51

sauces for pasta

Tomato-Garlic Sauce

Marinara Sauce

Roasted Summer Vegetable Sauce

Mushroom-Tomato Sauce

Peperonata Sauce

Pine Nut and Olive Sauce

Creamy Tomato-Peppers Sauce

Basil-Chive Pesto and Pasta

Puttanesca Sauce

Eggplant-Mushroom Sauce

Meat Sauce

Ricotta-Spinach Sauce

White Clam Sauce

TOMATO-GARLIC SAUCE

This flavorful sauce is easy to double or triple and works well with a variety of pasta shapes. You can keep it in the refrigerator for 3 or 4 days or freeze portions for later use.

- 2 tablespoons dry sherry, *or* chicken broth
- 1 tablespoon olive oil
- 2 teaspoons minced garlic
- 1 14½-ounce can diced tomatoes, including juice
- 1 15-ounce can Italian-seasoned tomato sauce
- 2 teaspoons granulated sugar
  Salt and pepper to taste

In a large, heavy saucepan, combine sherry, oil, and garlic. Cook over medium-low heat, stirring frequently, until garlic is golden, 5 to 7 minutes. Add tomatoes, tomato sauce, sugar, and salt and pepper, if desired. Bring to a boil. Cover, reduce heat, and simmer 20 to 25 minutes.

Serve over 8 to 10 ounces of penne or other pasta. Garnish with chopped parsley or grated Parmesan cheese, if desired.

PREPARATION TIME:
8 minutes
COOKING TIME:
25 minutes
SERVINGS: **4**

PER SERVING:
Calories: 96
Protein (g): 2.9
Carbohydrates (g): 14.1
Fat (g): 3.5
Saturated Fat (g): 0.5
Cholesterol (mg): 0
Dietary Fiber (g): 2.3
Sodium (mg): 817

MARINARA SAUCE

Of course you can buy marinara sauce in a jar. If you'd like to make your own, here's a full-bodied basic sauce that's good over plain pasta and can also be served with stuffed shells or over chicken or pork. If you like, double the recipe.

PREPARATION TIME:

15 minutes

COOKING TIME:

32 minutes

SERVINGS: *5*

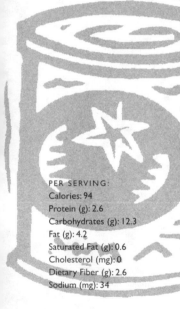

PER SERVING:
Calories: 94
Protein (g): 2.6
Carbohydrates (g): 12.3
Fat (g): 4.2
Saturated Fat (g): 0.6
Cholesterol (mg): 0
Dietary Fiber (g): 2.6
Sodium (mg): 34

1½ tablespoons olive oil, preferably extra-virgin
1 small onion, chopped
1 teaspoon minced garlic
1 15-ounce can reduced-sodium diced tomatoes, including juice
1 15-ounce can reduced-sodium, *or* regular, tomato sauce
3 tablespoons finely chopped fresh basil leaves
½ teaspoon dried oregano leaves
1 large bay leaf
Salt and pepper to taste

In a very large saucepan or pot, over medium-high heat, combine oil and onion. Adjust heat so onion browns but doesn't burn, and cook, stirring, until lightly browned, about 5 minutes. Add garlic and cook 2 minutes longer. Stir in tomatoes, tomato sauce, basil, oregano, and bay leaf.

Adjust heat so mixture simmers gently, and cook, uncovered and stirring occasionally, about 25 minutes. Discard bay leaf. Add salt and pepper, if desired.

Serve sauce over pasta or meat. If desired, top with grated Parmesan cheese.

ROASTED SUMMER VEGETABLE SAUCE

Roasting the vegetables gives this quick-and-easy sauce a rich flavor.
Microwaving them first speeds the cooking time.

PREPARATION TIME:
12 minutes
COOKING TIME:
22 minutes
SERVINGS: *7*

3	cups coarsely cut plum tomatoes
2	cups diced zucchini
1	cup very thinly sliced onion
1	red bell pepper, seeded and chopped
1½	tablespoons olive oil
½	teaspoon dried thyme leaves
	Salt and pepper to taste
1	8-ounce can tomato sauce

Preheat oven to 425 degrees. In an 8-cup measure or similar large microwave-safe bowl, combine tomatoes, zucchini, onion, pepper, oil, thyme, and salt and pepper, if desired. Toss to mix. Cover with wax paper, and microwave about 4 to 5 minutes.

Transfer vegetables to a large spray-coated baking pan, and bake for 18 to 20 minutes or until onion is tender. Stir in tomato sauce.

Serve over thin spaghetti, or toss with penne pasta.

PER SERVING:
Calories: 72
Protein (g): 2
Carbohydrates (g): 10.5
Fat (g): 3.4
Saturated Fat (g): 0.5
Cholesterol (mg): 0
Dietary Fiber (g): 2.7
Sodium (mg): 207

MUSHROOM-TOMATO SAUCE

The meaty taste of mushrooms comes through clearly in this simple yet substantial sauce. Serve it over pasta for a satisfying vegetarian main dish. Leftover sauce is also good spooned over steamed green beans, broccoli, or grilled chicken.

PREPARATION TIME:

12 minutes

COOKING TIME:

28 minutes

SERVINGS: 4

2   tablespoons olive oil, preferably extra-virgin
5½   cups coarsely sliced fresh mushrooms
1   large onion, finely chopped
1   teaspoon minced garlic
¼   cup dry red wine
1   28-ounce can reduced-sodium, *or* regular, Italian-style tomatoes, including juice, chopped
¼   cup tomato paste blended with ½ cup water
¾   teaspoon *each* dried thyme leaves and dried marjoram leaves
Salt and pepper to taste

In a 12-inch or larger non-stick saute pan or skillet, heat oil to hot, but not smoking, over medium-high heat. Add mushrooms, onion, and garlic; pan will initially be overfull, but mushrooms will gradually lose volume as they cook. Adjust heat so mushrooms and onion cook rapidly but do not burn, and cook, stirring, until juices evaporate and mushrooms are lightly browned, 7 to 9 minutes. Stir in wine, tomatoes, tomato paste—water mixture, thyme, and marjoram.

Adjust heat so mixture simmers, and cook, uncovered and stirring occasionally, about 20 minutes or until slightly thickened. Add salt and pepper, if desired. Serve sauce over pasta.

HELPFUL HINT:

If you particularly like the robust flavor of portobello mushrooms, use them instead of regular mushrooms. In this case, discard the stems (which are tough), and coarsely chop the caps into bite-size pieces.

PER SERVING:
Calories: 163
Protein (g): 5
Carbohydrates (g): 20.5
Fat (g): 7.6
Saturated Fat (g): 1
Cholesterol (mg): 0
Dietary Fiber (g): 4.7
Sodium (mg): 155

PEPERONATA SAUCE

This classic fresh bell pepper and tomato sauce is simple and tasty.

4   bell peppers (green, red, yellow, or a combination)
2   large onions, sliced
2   tablespoons olive oil
2   large ripe tomatoes, cut into large chunks (about $4\frac{1}{2}$ cups)
$\frac{1}{4}$ cup chicken broth
3   tablespoons tomato paste
2   tablespoons red wine vinegar
    Salt and pepper to taste

PREPARATION TIME:
12 minutes
COOKING TIME:
23 minutes
SERVINGS: *6*

Remove seeds and membranes from peppers, and cut them into thick strips. If desired, cut each strip in half crosswise. Set aside.

In a large, heavy pot, combine onions and oil. Cook over medium heat, stirring, until onions are just soft, 6 to 7 minutes. Add tomatoes, broth, and tomato paste, stirring to combine well. Stir in peppers. Add vinegar and salt and pepper to taste.

Cover, bring to a boil, and reduce heat. Simmer 15 to 18 minutes until peppers are just cooked. Remove pot cover, and simmer an additional 2 or 3 minutes to cook down slightly.

Serve over spaghetti or other pasta.

PER SERVING:
Calories: 90
Protein (g): 1.8
Carbohydrates (g): 11.3
Fat (g): 4.9
Saturated Fat (g): 0.7
Cholesterol (mg): 0
Dietary Fiber (g): 2.6
Sodium (mg): 113

PINE NUT AND OLIVE SAUCE

Quick and delicious, this simple sauce combines several classic Italian ingredients: pine nuts, tomatoes, olives, and garlic.

PREPARATION TIME:

12 minutes

COOKING TIME:

10 minutes

SERVINGS: 4

1 large onion, chopped

1 teaspoon minced garlic

$^1/_4$ cup dry sherry, *or* white wine

20 pitted black olives, sliced

$^1/_4$ cup pine nuts

1 15-ounce can Italian-seasoned diced tomatoes

1 8-ounce can reduced-sodium, *or* regular, tomato sauce

$^1/_8$ teaspoon black pepper

In a non-stick skillet, combine onion, garlic, and sherry. Cook over medium heat, stirring frequently, until onion is tender, 5 or 6 minutes.

Add olives, nuts, tomatoes, tomato sauce, and pepper. Reduce heat and simmer, covered, an additional 7 or 8 minutes.

Serve over pasta.

HELPFUL HINT:

You can make this recipe with pine nuts straight out of the package. But the sauce will taste more flavorful if you toast the pine nuts. To toast, spread them in a small non-stick skillet, and cook over medium heat, stirring frequently with a wooden spoon, for 4 or 5 minutes until nuts begin to brown. Remove at once to a plate and reserve.

PER SERVING:
Calories: 154
Protein (g): 5
Carbohydrates (g): 15
Fat (g): 7.7
Saturated Fat (g): 1.1
Cholesterol (mg): 0
Dietary Fiber (g): 3.2
Sodium (mg): 733

CREAMY TOMATO-PEPPERS SAUCE

Quick, easy, and delicious—this sauce is so creamy you'd swear it's high in fat. But it's really quite low. The roasted red peppers can be purchased in jars at many grocery stores or specialty markets. Serve over penne or other pasta.

PREPARATION TIME:

8 minutes

COOKING TIME:

17 minutes

SERVINGS: **4**

2 tablespoons dry sherry, *or* chicken broth
1 tablespoon olive oil
1 medium onion, chopped
½ teaspoon minced garlic
1 15-ounce can Italian-seasoned tomato sauce
⅓ cup coarsely chopped bottled roasted sweet red peppers
2 teaspoons granulated sugar
¼ cup reduced-fat sour cream
  Salt and pepper to taste

In a small Dutch oven or similar pot, combine sherry, oil, onion, and garlic. Cook, stirring frequently, until onion is soft, 5 to 7 minutes.

Add tomato sauce, peppers, and sugar; stir to mix well. Bring to a boil. Cover, lower heat, and simmer 10 to 15 minutes, stirring occasionally. Turn off heat under pot. Stir in the sour cream until well combined. Warm over very low heat an additional 2 minutes. Add salt and pepper, if desired. Serve sauce over pasta.

HELPFUL HINT:

Chopped parsley makes a nice garnish for this sauce.

PER SERVING:
Calories: 115
Protein (g): 3.2
Carbohydrates (g): 14.7
Fat (g): 4.7
Saturated Fat (g): 1.5
Cholesterol (mg): 5
Dietary Fiber (g): 2.5
Sodium (mg): 602

BASIL-CHIVE PESTO AND PASTA

Pesto and pasta make a wonderfully satisfying, rich-tasting combination. I've toasted the pine nuts because taking this step significantly increases their flavor.

PREPARATION TIME:
10 minutes

COOKING TIME:
7 minutes

SERVINGS: **6 ($^3/_4$ cup)**

PESTO:

3	tablespoons pine nuts (about 1 ounce)
2	teaspoons chopped garlic
1$^1/_2$	cups packed fresh basil leaves
$^1/_3$	cup packed chopped fresh chives, *or* green onions
$^1/_4$	cup grated Parmesan cheese
1	tablespoon lemon juice
$^1/_4$	teaspoon salt, *or* more to taste
$^1/_4$	cup extra-virgin olive oil

PASTA:

12 ounces uncooked pasta, such as vermicelli or angel hair, cooked according to package directions, rinsed and drained

PER SERVING:
Calories: 338
Protein (g): 10.1
Carbohydrates (g): 44.1
Fat (g): 13.6
Saturated Fat (g): 2.4
Cholesterol (mg): 2.6
Dietary Fiber (g): 2.7
Sodium (mg): 161

Spread nuts in a small, non-stick skillet. Cook over medium-high heat, stirring constantly, until nuts begin to turn brown and smell toasted, 3 to 4 minutes. Immediately transfer to a plate and cool slightly.

Combine nuts, garlic, basil, chives, cheese, lemon juice, and salt in food processor bowl and process until finely minced. With processor on, slowly pour oil through food tube; process until well blended, stopping and scraping down sides of container once or twice. Transfer to a small bowl. To serve, toss pesto with pasta.

Pesto will keep tightly sealed in the refrigerator for 2 to 3 days.

PUTTANESCA SAUCE

There's nothing subtle or refined about this spicy sauce. This may account for the name puttanesca, *which means prostitute-style. Even if you don't normally bother with reduced-sodium tomatoes, consider trying them in the following recipe. Since both the ham and olives have a lot of sodium, the sauce may be too salty if regular canned tomatoes are used.*

PREPARATION TIME:
12 minutes
COOKING TIME:
26 minutes
SERVINGS: *6*

2½	tablespoons olive oil, preferably extra-virgin
3	large onions, chopped
2	teaspoons minced garlic
1	cup finely diced well-trimmed lean ham, *or* Canadian bacon
2	28-ounce cans reduced-sodium Italian-style tomatoes, including juice, chopped, *or* regular Italian-style tomatoes
¼	cup finely sliced pitted green olives
1½	tablespoons dried oregano leaves
⅛–¼	teaspoon dried hot red pepper flakes, *or* to taste
	Salt and pepper to taste

In a 4-quart or larger pot over medium-high heat, combine oil, onions, and garlic. Adjust heat so onions brown but do not burn, and cook, stirring, until they are golden, 6 or 7 minutes. Stir in ham, tomatoes, olives, oregano, red pepper flakes, and salt and pepper, if desired.

Adjust heat so mixture simmers gently and cook, uncovered and stirring occasionally to prevent sticking, about 20 minutes until thickened. Serve over vermicelli, spaghetti, or similar pasta.

PER SERVING:
Calories: 179
Protein (g): 9.5
Carbohydrates (g): 19.6
Fat (g): 8.3
Saturated Fat (g): 1.4
Cholesterol (mg): 12.8
Dietary Fiber (g): 4.9
Sodium (mg): 486

EGGPLANT-MUSHROOM SAUCE

Eggplant and mushrooms go well together in this robust sauce. Both vegetables have a hearty, meaty taste, so this makes a very satisfying vegetarian entree. You'll need a microwave oven for this recipe.

PREPARATION TIME:
15 minutes
COOKING TIME:
28 minutes
SERVINGS: *4*

1 medium eggplant, peeled and cut into $\frac{2}{3}$-inch cubes
2 tablespoons olive oil, divided
$2\frac{1}{2}$ cups coarsely sliced fresh mushrooms
1 small onion, finely chopped
1 teaspoon minced garlic
$\frac{1}{3}$ cup tomato paste
$1\frac{3}{4}$ cups vegetable broth, *or* chicken broth
2 tablespoons dry white wine, *or* alcohol-free white wine, *or* water
$\frac{3}{4}$ teaspoon dried marjoram leaves
Salt and pepper to taste

PER SERVING:
Calories: 148
Protein (g): 3.1
Carbohydrates (g): 19.4
Fat (g): 7.4
Saturated Fat (g): 1
Cholesterol (mg): 0
Dietary Fiber (g): 5.2
Sodium (mg): 538

Spread eggplant in a large microwave-safe pie plate. Sprinkle a tablespoon of water over eggplant. Cover plate with wax paper. Microwave on High power 3 to 4 minutes, stirring after 2 minutes, until pieces are barely tender when tested with a fork. Turn out into a colander; drain well. Pat dry with paper towels.

In a 12-inch or larger non-stick saute pan or skillet, heat 1 tablespoon oil to hot, but not smoking, over high heat. Add eggplant, and cook, stirring, until lightly browned, about 5 minutes; adjust heat as necessary to prevent burning. Turn out eggplant into a bowl and reserve.

In the same skillet, heat remaining 1 tablespoon oil to hot but not smoking. Add mushrooms, onion, and garlic. Cook, stirring, until mushrooms are lightly browned, about 5 minutes.

Combine tomato paste and broth in small bowl, stirring to mix well. Stir into mushroom mixture, along with wine, marjoram, and reserved eggplant.

Adjust heat so mixture simmers. Cook, uncovered and stirring occasionally, for 15 to 20 minutes or until mixture is slightly thickened and eggplant is tender when pierced with a fork. Add salt and pepper, if desired. Serve sauce over pasta.

MEAT SAUCE

If I'm in the mood to make my own meat sauce, I want it to be good, which is why I'm willing to go to a little extra work. And I also want to make a lot so I can use it for several meals.

PREPARATION TIME:
18 minutes
COOKING TIME:
1 hour
SERVINGS: *8–9*

1¼ pounds ground round of beef
3 cups chopped onions
1 cup coarsely chopped fresh mushrooms
1½ teaspoons chopped garlic
1 14½-ounce can chopped tomatoes, including juice
15 baby carrots, coarsely cut
3 15-ounce cans reduced-sodium, *or* regular, tomato sauce
3 tablespoons tomato paste
2 teaspoons granulated sugar
2 teaspoons dried thyme leaves
1½ teaspoons dried basil leaves
½ teaspoon dried oregano leaves
2 bay leaves
Salt and pepper to taste
Grated Parmesan cheese for garnish (optional)

In a large, heavy pot, combine ground round, onion, mushrooms, and garlic. Cook over medium heat, stirring frequently and breaking up meat with a spoon, until beef is browned.

Meanwhile, combine tomatoes and their juice and carrots in a food processor bowl. Process until vegetables are pureed, using on and off bursts to break up any large pieces.

Add vegetable mixture to meat mixture. Add tomato sauce, tomato paste, and sugar, stirring to mix well.

Add thyme, basil, oregano, bay leaves, and salt and pepper, if desired. Stir well. Bring to a boil, cover, reduce heat, and simmer 50 to 60 minutes, stirring frequently, until flavors are well blended. Remove and discard bay leaves.

Serve over spaghetti. Garnish with grated Parmesan cheese, if desired.

HELPFUL HINT:

The recipe calls for carrots because they add flavor to the sauce. However, you could substitute some peeled broccoli stems for part of the carrots. Instead of the pureed carrots, you could also substitute 2 large chopped celery stalks.

PER SERVING:
Calories: 172
Protein (g): 15.6
Carbohydrates (g): 22.3
Fat (g): 2.4
Saturated Fat (g): 0.8
Cholesterol (mg): 30.5
Dietary Fiber (g): 4.5
Sodium (mg): 185

RICOTTA-SPINACH SAUCE

Simple but surprisingly good and satisfying. For best results, use a top-quality brand of frozen spinach. Serve this sauce over radiatore (radial-shaped) or other pasta.

PREPARATION TIME:
15 minutes
COOKING TIME:
13 minutes
SERVINGS: *5*

 2 10-ounce packages frozen spinach, thawed
 2 tablespoons olive oil, preferably extra-virgin
 2 cups sliced fresh mushrooms
 1 medium-sized onion, finely chopped
 1 1/2 teaspoons minced garlic
 1 1/4 cups reduced-sodium, *or* regular, chicken broth, *or* vegetable broth
 1 teaspoon *each* dried thyme leaves and dried marjoram leaves
 1/4 teaspoon ground nutmeg
 1 cup reduced-fat ricotta cheese
 1/2 cup grated Parmesan cheese
    Salt and pepper to taste

A handful at a time, squeeze excess moisture from spinach. Put spinach in a medium-sized bowl. Fluff it with a fork, discarding any tough stem pieces. If spinach is not finely chopped, transfer to a cutting board and chop finely.

In a 12-inch or larger non-stick saute pan or skillet, heat oil to hot, but not smoking, over high heat. Add mushrooms and onion. Adjust heat so mushrooms and onions cook rapidly but do not burn, and cook, stirring, 4 minutes. Add garlic and continue cooking until mushrooms are lightly browned, about 3 minutes longer. Stir in broth, spinach, thyme, marjoram, and nutmeg.

Adjust heat so mixture simmers, and cook, uncovered, stirring occasionally, 5 to 8 minutes or until spinach is tender. Stir in ricotta and Parmesan. Lower heat and cook just until piping hot; do not boil. Add salt and pepper, if desired. Toss sauce with fresh-cooked pasta and serve.

HELPFUL HINT:

While the recipe is best made with chicken broth, you can substitute vegetable broth if serving vegetarians.

PER SERVING:
Calories: 183
Protein (g): 11.3
Carbohydrates (g): 11.4
Fat (g): 10.8
Saturated Fat (g): 3.8
Cholesterol (mg): 18.3
Dietary Fiber (g): 3.4
Sodium (mg): 271

WHITE CLAM SAUCE

It's easy to get a quick, tempting meal on the table if you keep a couple of cans of minced clams on hand. While the sauce cooks, prepare some linguine or similar pasta.

PREPARATION TIME:

10 minutes

COOKING TIME:

15 minutes

SERVINGS: *4*

1 tablespoon olive oil, preferably extra-virgin

1 small onion, finely chopped

1$\frac{1}{2}$ teaspoons minced garlic

2 10$\frac{1}{4}$-ounce cans minced baby clams, including juice

$\frac{1}{3}$ cup dry white wine, *or* alcohol-free white wine

$\frac{1}{2}$ cup finely chopped fresh parsley leaves

1 teaspoon *each* dried oregano, dried marjoram, and dried basil leaves

1 tablespoon butter, *or* non-diet soft margarine

Salt and white pepper to taste

In a 12-inch non-stick skillet over high heat, combine oil, onion, and garlic. Lower heat slightly and cook until onion turns translucent and golden, about 5 minutes. Drain juice from clams into skillet. Add wine, parsley, oregano, marjoram, and basil.

Adjust heat so mixture simmers. Cook, uncovered and stirring occasionally, for 10 minutes. Add clams, butter, and salt and pepper, if desired. Heat until piping hot. Serve in large soup plates, spooned over hot cooked pasta.

PER SERVING:
Calories: 230
Protein (g): 23.9
Carbohydrates (g): 9.1
Fat (g): 10.9
Saturated Fat (g): 3.8
Cholesterol (mg): 124.4
Dietary Fiber (g): 1
Sodium (mg): 793

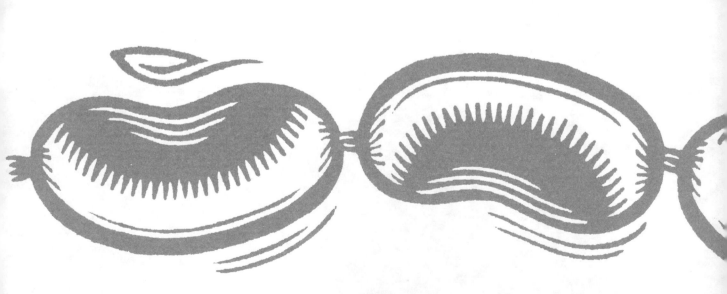

main dishes: meat

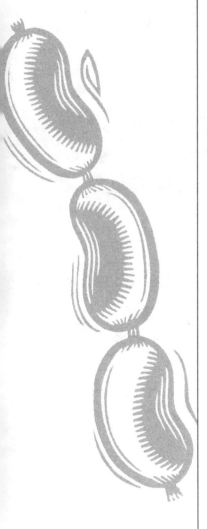

Grilled Beef and Peppers

Sicilian Beef and Rice

Round Steak Pizzaiola

Beef Braised in Red Wine

Spaghetti and Meatballs

Meatball Subs

Pork with Peppers and Onions

Sausage and Roasted Peppers Lasagne

Pepperoni-Vegetable-Pasta Skillet

GRILLED BEEF AND PEPPERS

Grilled meat and vegetables are served frequently in Italy. Here they're combined in a festive and flavorful presentation. To enrich the flavor, I cook the onions from the marinade with the peppers. If you like, the meat and vegetables can be served as sandwiches on lightly toasted Italian bread. Although the dish is very easy, you need to plan ahead, since the meat should be marinated for at least 12 hours.

PREPARATION TIME:

15 minutes

COOKING TIME:

15 minutes

SERVINGS: *4–6*

⅓	cup lemon juice
¼	cup chicken broth
3	tablespoons olive oil
1	large onion, coarsely chopped
1	tablespoon Italian seasoning
¼	teaspoon salt (optional)
3–4	drops hot pepper sauce
1–1½	pounds flank steak
3	bell peppers (preferably red, yellow, and green), seeded and sliced

In a shallow glass baking dish, combine lemon juice, broth, oil, onion, Italian seasoning, salt, if desired, and hot pepper sauce. Stir to mix well. Lay the meat in the baking dish. Spoon some of the marinade and onion over top. Cover and refrigerate 12 hours or up to 24 hours, turning and basting with marinade and onion once or twice.

Adjust rack 5 inches from broiler. Preheat broiler. Transfer meat to non-stick, spray-coated broiler pan. Broil meat 5 inches from heat for 11 to 16 minutes, turning once, until desired degree of doneness is reached.

Meanwhile, with a slotted spoon, remove onion from marinade and transfer to a non-stick skillet. Add peppers and 3 tablespoons of marinade. Cook over medium-high to high heat 4 or 5 minutes until onion and peppers begin to char.

To serve, slice meat on the diagonal, and arrange on a serving platter. Surround with peppers-onion mixture.

HELPFUL HINT:

You can marinate the meat a day or two before it's needed and keep it in the refrigerator. Marinating for 24 hours or longer will intensify the flavor.

Per serving:
Calories: 192
Protein (g): 18.9
Carbohydrates (g): 6.3
Fat (g): 10
Saturated Fat (g): 3.1
Cholesterol (mg): 31.3
Dietary Fiber (g): 1.2
Sodium (mg): 66

SICILIAN BEEF AND RICE

Instead of serving meat sauce with pasta, try this tasty variation that calls for rice.

PREPARATION TIME:
10 minutes
COOKING TIME:
25 minutes
SERVINGS: *4*

1	16-ounce bag frozen mixed pepper and onion stir-fry
1	teaspoon minced garlic
12	ounces ground round of beef
2	15-ounce cans reduced-sodium, *or* regular, tomato sauce
1½	teaspoons *each* dried basil leaves and dried thyme leaves
	Salt and pepper to taste
1	cup long-grain white rice
3	tablespoons grated Parmesan cheese

In a Dutch oven or similar large, heavy pot, combine pepper and onion mixture, garlic, and ground round. Cook, stirring frequently, over medium heat until beef has browned and onion is tender, 6 or 7 minutes.

Stir in tomato sauce, basil, thyme, and salt and pepper, if desired. Bring to a boil. Reduce heat and simmer, uncovered, for 18 to 20 minutes, stirring occasionally, until some of liquid has evaporated.

Meanwhile, cook rice according to package directions. (See Hint below.)

To serve, place cooked rice in a deep serving bowl. Ladle half of sauce over rice. Sprinkle with grated cheese. Toss gently with two forks until rice is mixed with sauce and cheese. Top individual portions with remaining sauce.

HELPFUL HINT:

For perfect rice, combine rice and hot water in a medium saucepan over high heat. Bring to a full boil, and boil, covered, for 1 minute before reducing heat to a simmer or very low boil. Then simmer, covered, for 19 more minutes. Uncover rice from time to time to check simmering action. As water cooks down, reduce heat further so that heat is very low by end of cooking process.

PER SERVING:
Calories: 407
Protein (g): 28
Carbohydrates (g): 62.2
Fat (g): 4.3
Saturated Fat (g): 1.8
Cholesterol (mg): 44.2
Dietary Fiber (g): 5.5
Sodium (mg): 170

ROUND STEAK PIZZAIOLA

I used to think we Americans made up the word "pizzaiola" until I enjoyed both steak and chicken prepared this way in several restaurants in northern Italy.

1–1¼ pounds round steak, trimmed of fat and cut into thin strips
⅛ teaspoon black pepper
1 large onion, chopped
¼ cup reduced-sodium, *or* regular, beef broth
1 tablespoon olive oil
2 15-ounce cans Italian-seasoned tomato sauce
12 ounces pasta, such as penne, cooked according to package directions
¼ cup grated Parmesan cheese

Sprinkle round steak with pepper. In a 12-inch non-stick skillet coated with non-stick spray, cook round steak over medium heat until browned on both sides, 4 to 5 minutes. Remove with a slotted spoon and reserve. In same skillet, combine onion, broth, and oil. Cook over medium heat, stirring frequently, until onion is tender, 5 to 6 minutes.

Return meat to skillet. Add tomato sauce. Stir to mix well. Bring to a boil. Reduce heat, cover, and simmer 35 to 40 minutes until meat is tender. Serve over pasta on individual plates. Sprinkle each serving with Parmesan cheese.

HELPFUL HINT:

If you like, you can add 2 to 3 cups of a fresh vegetable such as cauliflower florets or sliced zucchini to the meat and sauce after they have cooked for 15 minutes.

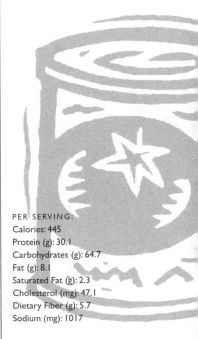

PREPARATION TIME:
10 minutes
COOKING TIME:
45 minutes
SERVINGS: **5**

PER SERVING:
Calories: 445
Protein (g): 30.1
Carbohydrates (g): 64.7
Fat (g): 8.1
Saturated Fat (g): 2.3
Cholesterol (mg): 47.1
Dietary Fiber (g): 5.7
Sodium (mg): 1017

BEEF BRAISED IN RED WINE

While this dish does take a little more time than most recipes in this book, the rich taste is worth the extra trouble. In Italy, it would be made with a pot roast. To shorten the cooking time, I've substituted beef round strips. A good quality Chianti works well in the recipe. However, you can substitute any table-quality dry red wine.

PREPARATION TIME:
20 minutes

COOKING TIME:
1 hour

SERVINGS: *6*

1½ pounds beef round steak, trimmed and cut into bite-size strips
 2 tablespoons all-purpose white flour
 1 large onion, chopped
 1 teaspoon minced garlic
 1 8-ounce package fresh mushrooms, sliced
 1 cup reduced-sodium beef broth, divided
 1 tablespoon olive oil
 2 large celery stalks, thinly sliced
10 large baby carrots
 1 15-ounce can reduced-sodium, *or* regular, tomato sauce
 1 cup dry red wine
 1 teaspoon dried thyme leaves
 2 large bay leaves
½ teaspoon dry mustard
   Salt and pepper to taste
⅛ teaspoon ground celery seed
 5 medium-sized baking potatoes, peeled and cut in halves

Preheat oven to 350 degrees.

In a large, shallow baking pan, combine beef and flour. Stir to coat meat. Bake for 12 to 15 minutes, stirring occasionally so that meat browns on all sides and any leftover flour coats meat. Remove and set aside.

Meanwhile, in a flameproof, ovenproof Dutch oven or similar large pot, combine onion, garlic, mushrooms, ¼ cup broth, and oil. Cook over medium heat, stirring frequently, until vegetables are tender, about 10 minutes.

Add celery and carrots along with tomato sauce, wine, remaining broth, and reserved beef. Add thyme, bay leaves, mustard, salt and pepper, if desired, and celery seed. Stir to mix well. Add potatoes, stirring them down into the sauce. Bring to a simmer. Cover, transfer pot to oven, and bake 45 to 50 minutes or until beef is tender. If desired, cut potato pieces in half before serving. Serve in large bowls.

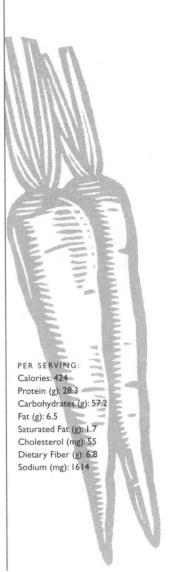

PER SERVING:
Calories: 424
Protein (g): 28.3
Carbohydrates (g): 57.2
Fat (g): 6.5
Saturated Fat (g): 1.7
Cholesterol (mg): 55
Dietary Fiber (g): 6.8
Sodium (mg): 1614

SPAGHETTI AND MEATBALLS

If you like your pasta dinners with meatballs, add these to your favorite sauce. They're easy to make because they brown in the oven.

MEATBALLS:

  1 pound ground round of beef
  ¼ cup packaged bread crumbs
  1 small onion, finely chopped
  1 teaspoon minced garlic
  2 teaspoons Italian seasoning
  1 large egg
  ½ teaspoon salt (optional)
  ⅛ teaspoon black pepper

SAUCE AND PASTA:

  6 cups (2, 26-ounce jars) pasta sauce
  16 ounces thin spaghetti

Preheat oven to 400 degrees.

In a large bowl, combine ground round, bread crumbs, onion, garlic, Italian seasoning, egg, salt, if desired, and pepper. Mix well. Roll into 30, 1-inch balls. Place balls in a shallow baking pan coated with non-stick spray. Bake for 10 to 15 minutes, stirring once, or until the meatballs are browned on all sides.

Heat sauce in a Dutch oven or similar large, heavy pot. When meatballs are browned, transfer to sauce and simmer 20 minutes.

Cook pasta according to package directions. Serve individual servings of meatballs and sauce over pasta.

PREPARATION TIME:
45 minutes
COOKING TIME:
30 minutes
SERVINGS: **6**

PER SERVING:
Calories: 573
Protein (g): 30.8
Carbohydrates (g): 88.2
Fat (g): 9.1
Saturated Fat (g): 1.4
Cholesterol (mg): 72
Dietary Fiber (g): 8.4
Sodium (mg): 1023

MEATBALL SUBS

For many families, meatball subs are a favorite lunch or light dinner entree. If you'd like to try them with easy, homemade meatballs, use the recipe on page 62. To round out the meal, I've topped the subs with vegetables cooked in the microwave.

1 recipe Meatballs (page 62)
1 26-ounce jar marinara sauce
1 cup sliced onions
2 cups sliced fresh mushrooms
1 small green bell pepper, seeded and chopped
½ teaspoon minced garlic
1 tablespoon water
6 6-inch submarine rolls
1⅛ cups reduced-fat shredded mozzarella cheese

Make the Meatballs according to recipe directions, except roll 24 slightly larger balls (1 rounded tablespoon each) and bake for 15 to 18 minutes, stirring once. Combine meatballs with sauce. Cover and simmer 10 to 15 minutes.

Meanwhile, place onions, mushrooms, pepper, garlic, and water in a microwave-safe medium bowl. Cover with wax paper, and microwave on High power about 5 to 6 minutes until vegetables are tender, stirring once during microwaving. Remove wax paper, and allow steam to escape. Drain liquid from vegetables.

Cut rolls lengthwise, and place each on an individual plate. Divide the meatball-sauce mixture evenly among the rolls, covering only one surface of each roll. Sprinkle 3 tablespoons of mozzarella over sauce and meatballs on each sandwich. Top with vegetable mixture, dividing it evenly. Close sandwiches. Serve with knives and forks.

PREPARATION TIME:

25 minutes

COOKING TIME:

18 minutes

SERVINGS: **6**

PER SERVING:
Calories: 683
Protein (gm): 36.2
Carbohydrates (gm): 94.5
Fat (gm): 19.6
Saturated Fat (gm): 5.8
Cholesterol (mg): 83.2
Dietary Fiber (g): 5.1
Sodium (mg): 1696

PORK WITH PEPPERS AND ONIONS

PREPARATION TIME:

12 minutes

COOKING TIME:

18 minutes

SERVINGS: *4–5*

Although this dish is traditionally served with whole pork chops, I've cut the pork into strips to speed the cooking time. If you'd like, you can add additional quick-cooking vegetables such as sliced zucchini or cauliflower florets in the last 15 minutes of cooking.

1 pound pork loin, trimmed of all fat and cut into strips
  Salt and pepper to taste
1 tablespoon olive oil
1 15-ounce can reduced-sodium, *or* regular, tomato sauce
1 16-ounce package frozen mixed pepper and onion stir-fry
2 tablespoons dry sherry
1 teaspoon minced garlic
1 teaspoon *each* dried basil and dried thyme leaves
8 ounces (2½ cups) cut fusilli, cooked according to package directions

Sprinkle pork with salt and pepper to taste, if desired. In a large non-stick skillet, cook pork strips in olive oil over medium heat, turning frequently, until they begin to brown, 4 to 6 minutes. With a slotted spoon remove to a medium bowl and set aside.

Add tomato sauce to pan and stir up any browned bits from pan bottom. Add pepper-onion mixture, sherry, garlic, basil, and thyme. Return pork to pan. Raise heat and bring to a boil. Cover, lower heat, and cook over medium heat, stirring occasionally, 12 to 15 minutes or until onions are almost tender.

Remove cover and simmer an additional 2 or 3 minutes to thicken sauce slightly. Taste sauce and add additional salt and pepper, if desired. Serve individual portions over pasta.

PER SERVING:
Calories: 364
Protein (g): 22.3
Carbohydrates (g): 46.9
Fat (g): 8.2
Saturated Fat (g): 2.2
Cholesterol (mg): 39.4
Dietary Fiber (g): 5.2
Sodium (mg): 71

SAUSAGE AND ROASTED PEPPERS LASAGNE

Like most lasagne recipes, this one takes a little time to assemble but is quite handy when you need a dish that can be made completely ahead and then simply reheated. Served along with a green salad and bread, it makes a very tempting, fuss-free meal.

PREPARATION TIME:

30 minutes

COOKING TIME:

51 minutes

SERVINGS: **12**

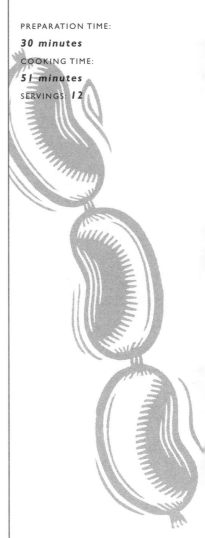

1	pound hot Italian sausage, casings removed and discarded
1	small onion, chopped
1	12-ounce jar roasted red sweet peppers, well-drained
6	cups homemade, *or* commercial (2, 26-ounce jars), meatless pasta sauce
1	15-ounce can Italian-seasoned chunky tomato sauce
2	15-ounce cartons part-skim ricotta cheese
1/2	cup liquid egg substitute, *or* 2 lightly beaten large eggs
2	cups shredded part-skim mozzarella cheese, divided
1/4	teaspoon *each* salt and pepper, *or* to taste
12	ounces lasagne noodles, cooked barely *al dente* and drained

Preheat oven to 375 degrees. Lightly spray a 4-quart (10- by 15-inch or similar) flat casserole or lasagne pan with non-stick spray.

In a very large, deep-sided skillet or saute pan over high heat, combine sausage and onion. Adjust heat so mixture cooks briskly but does not burn. Cook, breaking up meat as much as possible with a spoon, until it is nicely browned, 6 to 8 minutes. Discard all fat from skillet.

Coarsely chop roasted peppers, discarding any bits of skin. Stir peppers, pasta sauce, and seasoned tomatoes into skillet. Simmer mixture about 5 minutes; set aside.

In a large bowl, stir together ricotta, egg substitute, half of mozzarella, and salt and pepper; reserve remaining mozzarella for topping.

Spread some sauce in casserole bottom. Top with 1/3 of noodles, then with 1/2 of ricotta mixture. Top with a layer of sauce. Repeat layering with 1/3 of noodles, remainder of ricotta mixture, then half of remaining sauce. Top with remaining noodles, then remaining sauce; dish will be full.

Place lasagne dish on a large baking sheet to catch drips. Bake for 40 to 50 minutes until bubbly and cooked through. If serving immediately, sprinkle reserved mozzarella cheese over top and let lasagne stand until mozzarella melts, about 5 minutes. If serving reheated, add mozzarella after lasagne is rewarmed. To serve, cut lengthwise in half, then crosswise into sevenths.

HELPFUL HINT:

The lasagne may be made several days ahead. Reheat in a preheated 325-degree oven for 35 to 45 minutes before serving. If the top begins to dry out, cover the dish with foil during reheating.

PER SERVING:
Calories: 419
Protein (g): 23.5
Carbohydrates (g): 28.6
Fat (g): 23.1
Saturated Fat (g): 9.2
Cholesterol (mg): 63.7
Dietary Fiber (g): 3.2
Sodium (mg): 1297

PEPPERONI-VEGETABLE-PASTA SKILLET

For convenience, buy a 3-ounce, pre-sliced package of pepperoni and cut-up, ready-to-use broccoli florets.

1¼ cups uncooked small macaroni
1 tablespoon olive oil
1 large onion, coarsely chopped
½ cup coarsely chopped red bell pepper
1 teaspoon minced garlic
3–4 ounces sliced pepperoni, coarsely diced
⅓ cup reduced-sodium, *or* regular, chicken broth
1 14½-ounce can Italian-style tomatoes, including juice, chopped
¾ teaspoon *each* dried oregano leaves and dried marjoram leaves
3 cups broccoli florets
Salt and pepper to taste
1–2 tablespoons grated Parmesan cheese for garnish (optional)

PREPARATION TIME:
12 minutes
COOKING TIME:
20 minutes
SERVINGS: *4*

Cook macaroni according to package directions until barely *al dente*. Rinse under cold water and drain.

Meanwhile, in a 12-inch or larger non-stick saute pan or skillet, heat oil to hot, but not smoking, over high heat. Add onion, bell pepper, and garlic. Lower heat slightly, and cook, stirring, until vegetables are lightly browned, about 5 minutes.

Add pepperoni, broth, tomatoes, oregano, and marjoram; simmer 10 minutes. Stir in broccoli, and cook until almost tender, 4 to 5 minutes longer. Stir in macaroni. Simmer several minutes longer until broccoli is cooked through and flavors have blended. Add salt and pepper, if desired. Garnish servings with Parmesan, if desired.

PER SERVING:
Calories: 319
Protein (g): 12.3
Carbohydrates (g): 37.6
Fat (g): 13.8
Saturated Fat (g): 4.1
Cholesterol (mg): 16.8
Dietary Fiber (g): 4.3
Sodium (mg): 968

main dishes: poultry

Tuscan Chicken

Chicken Risotto

Chicken Breasts with Rosemary

Chicken-Pasta Skillet with Sun-Dried Tomatoes and Olives

Easy Crisp-Baked Herbed Chicken Breasts

Turkey Cacciatore

Turkey Cutlets with Sage

Turkey Marsala with Mushrooms

TUSCAN CHICKEN

Although this chicken dish is rich with the hearty flavors of country Tuscan cooking, I've simplified the recipe considerably for ease and efficiency.

1 1-ounce package dried porcini mushrooms
1 cup reduced-sodium, *or* regular, chicken broth
6 boneless, skinless chicken breast halves
2 tablespoons white flour
2 tablespoons olive oil
$^1/_2$ cup dry white wine
1 $14^1/_2$-ounce can Italian-seasoned tomato sauce
$^1/_4$ teaspoon black pepper

In a 2-cup glass measure or similar microwave-safe bowl, combine mushrooms and broth. Stir to make sure all the mushrooms are wet. Cover with wax paper, and microwave on High power about 4 or $4^1/_2$ minutes or until mushrooms are reconstituted. Drain mushrooms through a fine sieve or coffee filter, reserving the broth. Wash mushrooms, and cut up any large pieces.

Coat chicken pieces with flour.

Place oil in a large non-stick skillet. Add chicken pieces, in batches if necessary, and brown them on both sides over medium heat. Stir in wine, tomato sauce, and black pepper. Add broth and mushrooms. Cover, reduce heat, and simmer 25 minutes until chicken is tender. Remove lid, raise heat slightly, and cook down sauce until it has thickened slightly, about 5 minutes.

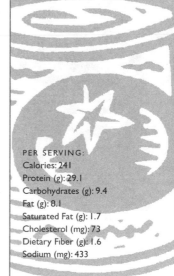

PREPARATION TIME:
18 minutes
COOKING TIME:
35 minutes
SERVINGS: *6*

PER SERVING:
Calories: 241
Protein (g): 29.1
Carbohydrates (g): 9.4
Fat (g): 8.1
Saturated Fat (g): 1.7
Cholesterol (mg): 73
Dietary Fiber (g): 1.6
Sodium (mg): 433

CHICKEN RISOTTO

For this dish, start with the Risotto recipe on page 102. While it's cooking, prepare the chicken and vegetables.

PREPARATION TIME:

20 minutes

COOKING TIME:

16 minutes

SERVINGS: *5–6*

1 recipe Microwave Risotto (page 102)

12 ounces boneless, skinless chicken breast halves, trimmed and cut into small bite-size pieces

Salt and pepper to taste

1 teaspoon dried thyme leaves, divided

1 tablespoon olive oil

$\frac{1}{4}$ cup reduced-sodium, *or* regular, chicken broth

$\frac{1}{4}$ cup dry white wine, *or* sherry

$\frac{1}{2}$ teaspoon dried oregano leaves

2 cups frozen mixed peppers and onion stir-fry

Prepare risotto, omitting Parmesan cheese.

Meanwhile, prepare the chicken and vegetables. Sprinkle chicken with salt and pepper, if desired, and $\frac{1}{2}$ teaspoon thyme. In a 12-inch non-stick skillet, combine chicken and oil. Cook over medium heat, turning chicken pieces frequently until they begin to brown, 4 to 5 minutes.

Add broth, wine, remaining thyme, and oregano. Stir in frozen peppers and onion. Bring to a boil, reduce heat, cover, and simmer 12 to 15 minutes. Stir chicken mixture into risotto and serve.

PER SERVING:

Calories: 243

Protein (g): 15.6

Carbohydrates (g): 21.8

Fat (g): 9.1

Saturated Fat (g): 3.8

Cholesterol (mg): 45.4

Dietary Fiber (g): 1.5

Sodium (mg): 97

CHICKEN BREASTS WITH ROSEMARY

Easy yet elegant, this zesty, healthful entree is good served along with a risotto and simple vegetable dish or salad. If you use dried rosemary, be sure to crumble or chop the needles very finely to help them soften and permeate the seasoning mixture with their flavor.

PREPARATION AND MARINATION TIME:

20 minutes

COOKING TIME:

21 minutes

SERVINGS: **4**

1	tablespoon olive oil, divided
1½	teaspoons balsamic vinegar
1	teaspoon minced garlic
	Zest (yellow part of peel), finely grated, of 1 medium-sized lemon
¼	teaspoon salt
⅛	teaspoon pepper
4	boneless, skinless chicken breast halves (4½ ounces each)
⅓	cup dry white wine, *or* alcohol-free white wine, *or* chicken broth
¼	teaspoon finely chopped fresh rosemary, *or* ½ teaspoon finely crumbled dried rosemary
½	cup peeled and diced fresh tomato

In a medium-sized bowl, stir together ½ tablespoon oil, vinegar, garlic, lemon zest, salt, and pepper. Stir in chicken; let stand for 10 minutes.

In a 12-inch skillet or saute pan, heat remaining oil over medium-high heat until very hot but not smoking. Add chicken pieces and any remaining seasoning mixture. Adjust heat so chicken sears and cooks rapidly but does not burn. Cook, turning frequently, until well-browned on all sides, 5 to 7 minutes.

Add wine and rosemary to skillet. Lower heat so mixture simmers gently. Cook 10 minutes; if necessary add 2 or 3 tablespoons water to prevent skillet from boiling dry. Add tomatoes and continue gently simmering until chicken is just cooked through, 6 to 8 minutes longer. If skillet is nearly dry, stir in several tablespoons of water to produce a little sauce. Serve with some tomato and sauce spooned over chicken pieces.

PER SERVING:
Calories: 205
Protein (g): 28.7
Carbohydrates (g): 2.5
Fat (g): 6.7
Saturated Fat (g): 1.4
Cholesterol (mg): 77.6
Dietary Fiber (g): 0.5
Sodium (mg): 217

CHICKEN-PASTA SKILLET WITH SUN-DRIED TOMATOES AND OLIVES

Sun-dried tomatoes and oil-cured black olives lend a rich, earthy flavor to this colorful one-dish meal. If you happen to have leftover cooked rigatoni, ziti, or other sturdy tube-shaped pasta on hand, use $2\frac{2}{3}$ cups of it to replace the uncooked pasta called for.

PREPARATION TIME:

15 minutes

COOKING TIME:

15 minutes

SERVINGS: **5**

$1\frac{1}{2}$ cups (about 4 ounces) uncooked rigatoni, *or* other medium tube-shaped pasta

1 tablespoon extra-virgin olive oil

$\frac{1}{2}$ cup *each* chopped onion and green bell pepper

1 pound boneless, skinless chicken breast halves, cut into 1-inch pieces

1 large zucchini, coarsely cubed

$1\frac{1}{2}$ cups Italian-seasoned chunky-style canned tomatoes

1 teaspoon dried marjoram leaves

3 tablespoons diced oil-packed sun-dried tomatoes

2 tablespoons chopped, pitted, oil-cured black olives, *or* Greek black olives

Salt and pepper to taste

PER SERVING:

Calories: 262
Protein (g): 24.5
Carbohydrates (g): 23.9
Fat (g): 7.3
Saturated Fat (g): 1.3
Cholesterol (mg): 55.2
Dietary Fiber (g): 2.1
Sodium (mg): 532

Cook the pasta according to package directions barely *al dente* and drain.

Meanwhile, in a 12-inch non-stick skillet, combine oil, onion, and pepper over medium-high heat. Cook, stirring, for about 4 minutes or until onions soften. Stir in chicken and cook, stirring, about 3 minutes longer until chicken pieces are almost cooked through. Stir in zucchini, tomatoes, marjoram, sun-dried tomatoes, olives, salt and pepper, if desired, and pasta until well mixed. Cook until bubbly hot and flavors are blended, 8 to 10 minutes longer.

EASY CRISP-BAKED HERBED CHICKEN BREASTS

Nothing could be easier than this simple Italian-seasoned shake-it, bake-it chicken entree.

PREPARATION TIME:
7 minutes
BAKING TIME:
40 minutes
SERVINGS: **4**

1   tablespoon olive oil
1   teaspoon butter, *or* non-diet soft margarine
1   teaspoon dried oregano leaves
¼   teaspoon (generous) garlic salt
⅛   teaspoon pepper
⅓   cup Italian-seasoned bread crumbs
4   boneless, skinless chicken breast halves (4½–5 ounces each)

Preheat oven to 400 degrees.

Put oil and butter in a 10-inch pie plate or similar-size flat baking dish. Place plate in the oven just until butter melts. Then remove, and tip plate back and forth to blend oil and butter; set aside.

In a large, sturdy paper or plastic bag, combine oregano, garlic salt, pepper, and bread crumbs. Shake until well mixed. Pat chicken breasts dry with paper towels. Add chicken pieces to bag. Shake until chicken pieces are well coated.

Place chicken in pie plate, reserving any crumbs remaining in bag. Pat down chicken lightly to coat with oil mixture. Turn over and pat down to coat other side. Sprinkle reserved bread crumb mixture over chicken.

Cover plate with aluminum foil and bake on center oven rack for 10 minutes. Remove foil; continue baking 30 to 35 minutes, until pieces are nicely browned and cooked through.

HELPFUL HINT:

Pop some baking potatoes into the oven as you're readying the chicken. Then you'll need only a vegetable side dish or salad to round out the meal.

PER SERVING:
Calories: 216
Protein (g): 26.2
Carbohydrates (g): 5.1
Fat (g): 8.1
Saturated Fat (g): 2.1
Cholesterol (mg): 80.3
Dietary Fiber (g): 0.4
Sodium (mg): 381

TURKEY CACCIATORE

Usually, turkey breast cutlets are used as is. Here, however, they are cut up into bite-sized pieces to make a very easy, quick-cooking cacciatore-style skillet.

PREPARATION TIME:

12 minutes

COOKING TIME:

21 minutes

SERVINGS: 4

   2 tablespoons olive oil
   ³⁄₄ cup *each* coarsely sliced fresh mushrooms and diced zucchini
   2 tablespoons all-purpose white flour
   ³⁄₄ teaspoon dried oregano leaves
   1 pound turkey breast cutlets, cut into 2-inch pieces
   1 14¹⁄₂-ounce can chunky "pasta-style" tomatoes, *or* "Italian recipe"
       stewed tomatoes
      Salt and pepper to taste

Combine oil, mushrooms, and zucchini in a 12-inch non-stick skillet over high heat. Adjust heat so vegetables cook briskly but do not burn. Cook, stirring, until they are lightly browned, about 5 minutes.

Combine flour and oregano in a medium-sized sturdy paper or plastic bag. Add turkey pieces and shake until they are coated with flour mixture. Transfer turkey pieces and any leftover flour to skillet.

Cook, stirring, until turkey just begins to brown, about 4 minutes longer. Stir in tomatoes and ¹⁄₃ cup water. Scrape up any flour from pan bottom. Adjust heat so the turkey simmers gently. Cook, uncovered, stirring occasionally, until mixture is slightly thickened and the flavors are well blended, 12 to 15 minutes longer. Add salt and pepper, if desired. Serve over hot pasta or rice (not included in nutritional data).

PER SERVING:
Calories: 218
Protein (g): 21.3
Carbohydrates (g): 8.8
Fat (g): 10.7
Saturated Fat (g): 1.6
Cholesterol (mg): 44.7
Dietary Fiber (g): 1.5
Sodium (mg): 585

TURKEY CUTLETS WITH SAGE

Sage is often paired with poultry in Italian cooking. It adds a robust flavor and aroma in this dish.

4   teaspoons red wine vinegar
2   large garlic cloves, smashed and chopped
2   teaspoons dried sage leaves, finely crumbled
1   pound turkey breast cutlets
     Salt and pepper to taste
4   tablespoons all-purpose white flour, divided
1   tablespoon olive oil, divided
2   teaspoons butter, *or* non-diet soft margarine, divided
½   cup reduced-sodium, *or* regular, chicken broth
1   tablespoon lemon juice

PREPARATION TIME:
15 minutes
COOKING TIME:
12 minutes
SERVINGS: *4*

Lay out a large sheet of plastic wrap. Sprinkle half of vinegar, half of garlic, and half of sage on plastic wrap. Lay cutlets on plastic wrap. Sprinkle remaining vinegar, garlic, and sage over cutlets. Season with salt and pepper, if desired. Cover cutlets with second sheet of plastic wrap. Using a kitchen mallet or back of a large, heavy spoon, pound cutlets to flatten them and embed the garlic and sage. Let stand 5 minutes.

Transfer cutlets to a clean sheet of plastic wrap. Dust with half of flour. Turn over and dust with remaining flour. Preheat oven to 200 degrees.

In a 12-inch non-stick skillet, heat ½ tablespoon oil and 1 teaspoon butter over medium-high heat until hot but not smoking. Add half of cutlets. Cook on one side until lightly browned, about 1½ minutes. Turn over and cook on second side until browned and just cooked through, 2 to 3 minutes longer. Transfer cutlets to an ovenproof serving dish. Cover and hold in oven.

Add remaining oil and remaining butter to skillet. Heat until hot. Add remaining cutlets. Repeat cooking process with second batch. Transfer cutlets to oven.

Stir broth and lemon juice into skillet. Cook over high heat, stirring, until liquid is reduced by half, 2 to 3 minutes. Pour mixture over cutlets. Serve immediately.

PER SERVING:
Calories: 186
Protein (g): 20.6
Carbohydrates (g): 7
Fat (g): 7.9
Saturated Fat (g): 2.5
Cholesterol (mg): 50.2
Dietary Fiber (g): 0.4
Sodium (mg): 68

TURKEY MARSALA WITH MUSHROOMS

In this recipe, turkey cutlets stand in for veal with great results. The directions call for smashing the garlic cloves before chopping so their juice can be pressed into the turkey more readily.

PREPARATION TIME:
15 minutes
COOKING TIME:
18 minutes
SERVINGS: **4**

1 pound turkey breast cutlets

2 teaspoons lemon juice

2 large garlic cloves, peeled, smashed, and chopped
 Salt and pepper to taste

4 tablespoons all-purpose white flour, divided

3 teaspoons olive oil, divided

3 teaspoons butter, divided

$\frac{1}{4}$ cup finely chopped onion

2 cups coarsely sliced fresh mushrooms

$\frac{1}{2}$ cup dry Marsala wine

$\frac{1}{2}$ cup reduced-sodium, *or* regular, chicken broth
 Chopped fresh parsley leaves and lemon wedges for garnish (optional)

Lay cutlets on sheet of plastic wrap. Sprinkle with lemon juice. Sprinkle garlic over cutlets. Cover cutlets with second sheet of plastic wrap. Using a kitchen mallet or back of a large, heavy spoon, pound each cutlet until $\frac{1}{8}$ inch thick. Let stand 5 minutes.

Lay cutlets on clean plastic wrap or wax paper. Season with salt and pepper. Dust with half of flour. Turn over and season second side; then dust with remaining flour. Preheat oven to 200 degrees.

In a 12-inch non-stick skillet, heat 1 teaspoon oil and 1 teaspoon butter over medium-high heat until hot but not smoking. Add half of cutlets. Cook on one side until lightly browned, about $1\frac{1}{2}$ minutes. Turn over and cook on second side until lightly browned and just cooked through, about 2 minutes longer. Transfer cutlets to an ovenproof serving dish. Cover and let stand in oven. Add 1 teaspoon more oil and 1 teaspoon more butter to skillet. Heat until hot. Add remaining cutlets. Repeat cooking process with second batch. Transfer cutlets to oven.

Add remaining teaspoon oil and butter, then onion and mushrooms, to skillet. Adjust heat so mixture cooks rapidly and cook, stirring, for 4 to 6 minutes or until mushrooms are browned and most juice has evaporated from pan.

Stir wine and broth into pan. Cook over highest heat, stirring, until liquid is reduced by half, about 3 minutes. Remove cutlets from oven. Pour mushroom mixture over them. Garnish with parsley, if desired. Serve immediately, along with lemon wedges, if desired.

PER SERVING:
Calories: 227
Protein (g): 21.5
Carbohydrates (g): 9.6
Fat (g): 9.1
Saturated Fat (g): 3.2
Cholesterol (mg): 52.9
Dietary Fiber (g): 0.9
Sodium (mg): 81

main dishes: fish

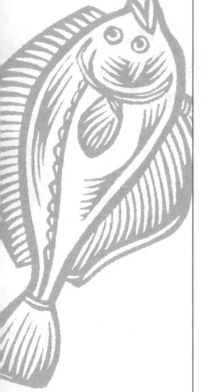

Tuna Steaks with Sweet-and-Sour Tomato-Basil Relish

Salmon Risotto

Sole, Mediterranean Style

Florentine Fish Dinner

Baked Stuffed Fish with Wine

Braised Fish with Sun-Dried Tomato Sauce

Fish Stew Marsala

TUNA STEAKS WITH SWEET-AND-SOUR TOMATO-BASIL RELISH

Spicy tomato relish nicely complements grilled tuna in this easy but elegant recipe.

TUNA:

1	teaspoon olive oil
1/2	teaspoon minced garlic
1/2	teaspoon lemon juice
1/4	teaspoon *each* dried thyme and basil leaves
	Salt and pepper to taste
1	pound tuna steak

RELISH:

2	tablespoons tomato paste
1 1/2	tablespoons red wine vinegar
1/2	tablespoon water
1 1/2	tablespoons granulated sugar
1	teaspoon olive oil
1/4	teaspoon *each* dried thyme and basil leaves
1	large tomato, seeded and cubed

PREPARATION TIME:
15 minutes
COOKING TIME:
18 minutes
SERVINGS: *4*

Preheat broiler. In a small bowl, stir together oil, garlic, lemon juice, thyme, basil, and salt and pepper, if desired.

Coat a broiler pan with non-stick spray. Place fish on pan. Drizzle oil and lemon mixture over fish, and spread it evenly with the back of a spoon.

Broil fish about 5 inches from heat for 10 minutes. Turn with a broad spatula, and broil an additional 6 to 10 minutes or until flesh has turned white and is cooked all the way through.

Meanwhile, in a small bowl, combine tomato paste, vinegar, and water. Stir to mix well. Add sugar, oil, thyme, and basil. Set aside.

Just before fish is cooked, in a small non-stick skillet coated with non-stick spray, sear tomato briefly over high heat. Stir into sauce.

Serve tuna on individual plates or serving platter. Pass tomato relish.

PER SERVING:
Calories: 172
Protein (g): 26.1
Carbohydrates (g): 7.9
Fat (g): 3.5
Saturated Fat (g): 0.6
Cholesterol (mg): 49.4
Dietary Fiber (g): 1
Sodium (mg): 45

SALMON RISOTTO

This rich and flavorful entree makes a wonderful centerpiece for a company meal. Not only that, it's a real time-saver because you prepare the salmon and sauce while the risotto cooks in the microwave oven.

PREPARATION TIME:
10 minutes
COOKING TIME:
19 minutes
SERVINGS: *6*

RISOTTO:

- 1 cup uncooked arborio rice
- 2 teaspoons olive oil
- 3⅓ cups reduced-sodium, *or* regular, chicken broth

SALMON:

- 12–16 ounces Atlantic salmon fillet, cut into 4-inch pieces
- ½ cup 1% fat milk
- 1 cup reduced-fat sour cream
- 2 teaspoons dried dill, *or* 1 tablespoon fresh dill
- ¾ cup sliced green onions
- ¼ cup dry sherry
- Salt and pepper to taste

In a 3-quart, microwave-safe casserole, combine rice and oil. Microwave, uncovered, about 60 seconds on High power. Stir well. Add broth, and stir to mix well. Cover with casserole lid, and microwave about 8 to 9 minutes. Stir well. Microwave an additional 8 minutes. Stir. Uncover and microwave an additional 4 to 5 minutes or until most of liquid is absorbed and rice is tender. Allow to stand 2 to 3 minutes.

While risotto cooks, in a large non-stick skillet coated with non-stick spray, cook salmon over medium heat, breaking up large pieces, until cooked through, 9 to 11 minutes. Remove from the pan, remove skin, flake, and set aside.

In a 2-cup measure, combine milk and sour cream; whisk until smooth. Add dill and stir to mix. Set aside.

In pan in which salmon was cooked, combine onions and sherry. Cook over medium heat, stirring frequently, 1½ to 2 minutes, until onions are just cooked. Stir in milk mixture until well combined. Stir in reserved salmon. Cook over very low heat for 2 minutes, stirring frequently, until flavors are blended. Do not boil.

Stir salmon mixture into risotto. Add salt and pepper, if desired. Garnish with dill sprigs or chopped fresh parsley, if desired.

PER SERVING:
Calories: 317
Protein (g): 17.6
Carbohydrates (g): 31.9
Fat (g): 10.1
Saturated Fat (g): 4.1
Cholesterol (mg): 44.3
Dietary Fiber (g): 1.1
Sodium (mg): 85

SOLE, MEDITERRANEAN STYLE

The recipe for this fast and flavorful fish dinner features sole, but you can substitute any lean, mild-flavored white fish such as flounder, halibut, or turbot. Directions call for cooking the vegetables and then the fish in the same skillet. For speedier dinner preparation, the fish can be prepared in a separate skillet while the vegetables are cooking.

PREPARATION TIME:

7 minutes

COOKING TIME:

13 minutes

SERVINGS: **4**

- ½ cup dry-packed sun-dried tomatoes
- 7–9 ounces uncooked penne, *or* other similar pasta shape
- 1 16-ounce bag frozen mixed pepper and onion stir-fry
- ½ cup reduced-sodium, *or* regular, chicken broth
- 2 teaspoons olive oil
- 1 teaspoon minced garlic
- 1 teaspoon dried basil leaves
- ¼ cup grated Parmesan cheese
  Salt and pepper to taste
- 12–16 ounces fresh, *or* frozen (thawed), skinless fillets of sole

In a 1-cup measure or similar bowl, cover tomatoes with hot water, and let stand 5 to 10 minutes. Drain and chop.

Cook pasta according to package directions. Rinse and drain in a colander.

Meanwhile, in a 12-inch non-stick skillet, combine pepper-onion mixture, broth, reserved tomatoes, oil, garlic, and basil. Stir to mix well. Cook, uncovered, over medium to medium-high heat 10 to 12 minutes, stirring frequently, until onions are very tender. Stir in Parmesan. Stir pasta into vegetable mixture. Transfer to serving platter, and keep warm.

Rinse out and dry skillet in which vegetables were cooked. Spray-coat with non-stick spray. Sprinkle fish with salt and pepper, if desired.

In batches, if necessary, add fish to pan, and cook over medium heat until cooked through, 3 to 6 minutes, depending on thickness.

Top pasta-vegetable mixture with fish and serve.

PER SERVING:
Calories: 360
Protein (g): 26.9
Carbohydrates (g): 48
Fat (g): 6.2
Saturated Fat (g): 1.8
Cholesterol (mg): 49
Dietary Fiber (g): 5.4
Sodium (mg): 331

FLORENTINE FISH DINNER

I like to make this quick and easy recipe with flounder, but you can substitute any mild-flavored white fish such as sole, halibut, or turbot.

PREPARATION TIME:

10 minutes

COOKING TIME:

12 minutes

SERVINGS: *4–5*

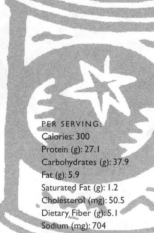

PER SERVING:
Calories: 300
Protein (g): 27.1
Carbohydrates (g): 37.9
Fat (g): 5.9
Saturated Fat (g): 1.2
Cholesterol (mg): 50.5
Dietary Fiber (g): 5.1
Sodium (mg): 704

9   ounces linguine, cooked according to package directions
1   pound skinless mild white fish fillets
    Salt and pepper to taste
1   14-ounce can Italian-seasoned chunky tomato sauce
2   cups cut-leaf frozen spinach
1   tablespoon olive oil
1/2 teaspoon minced garlic
    Salt and pepper to taste
3   tablespoons grated Parmesan cheese

Preheat oven to 200 degrees.

Cook linguine according to package directions.

Spray-coat a non-stick skillet with non-stick spray. Sprinkle salt and pepper over fish, if desired.

In batches, if necessary, add fish to skillet, and cook over medium heat until cooked through, 2 to 4 minutes per side, depending on thickness. Remove fish from pan, and set aside in oven to keep warm.

Rinse out and dry skillet in which fish was cooked. In skillet, combine tomato sauce, spinach, oil, garlic, and salt and pepper, if desired. Stir to mix well. Bring to a boil. Lower heat, cover, and cook 6 to 8 minutes or until flavors are well blended and spinach is done.

To serve, arrange cooked pasta on a serving platter. Top with tomato-spinach mixture and then reserved fish. Sprinkle Parmesan over all.

BAKED STUFFED FISH WITH WINE

Here's a quick and easy fish dinner that starts the vegetables in the microwave to reduce their preparation time.

1	large onion, chopped
1/2	teaspoon minced garlic
6	ounces fresh mushrooms, sliced (about 2 1/2 cups)
2	tablespoons chicken broth
1 1/2	cups crumb-type seasoned stuffing mix
3	tablespoons grated Parmesan cheese
1	pound lean white fish
1/4	teaspoon dried basil leaves
	Salt and pepper to taste
1/4	cup dry white wine

Preheat oven to 375 degrees.

In a 2 1/2-quart, microwave-safe, ovenproof casserole, stir together onion, garlic, mushrooms, and chicken broth. Cover with casserole lid. Microwave on High power about 5 to 6 minutes, or until onion is tender; stop and stir once during microwaving. Remove from microwave and stir in stuffing mix and Parmesan.

Sprinkle fish with basil and salt and pepper, if desired. Arrange fish on top of stuffing mixture, cutting to fit, and overlapping pieces of fish if necessary. Pour wine over fish. Cover and bake for 20 to 25 minutes or until fish flakes easily with a fork.

PREPARATION TIME:

12 minutes

COOKING TIME:

25 minutes

SERVINGS: 4

PER SERVING:
Calories: 214
Protein (g): 26
Carbohydrates (g): 16.9
Fat (g): 3.3
Saturated Fat (g): 1.2
Cholesterol (mg): 63.2
Dietary Fiber (g): 1.8
Sodium (mg): 426

BRAISED FISH WITH SUN-DRIED TOMATO SAUCE

The combination of tomato sauce and sun-dried tomatoes gives this dish rich color and flavor. It's quick and easy to prepare.

PREPARATION TIME:

10 minutes

COOKING TIME:

14 minutes

SERVINGS: *4*

1 tablespoon olive oil

1 teaspoon minced garlic

1 large onion, chopped

1 cup bottled clam juice, *or* reduced-sodium, *or* regular, chicken broth

3 tablespoons chopped oil-packed sun-dried tomatoes

1 teaspoon dried marjoram leaves

1/2 teaspoon dried oregano leaves

1 1/4 pounds fresh, *or* frozen, boneless, skinless halibut, red snapper, *or* similar firm white-fleshed fish, cut into 4 serving pieces

1 8-ounce can reduced-sodium, *or* regular, tomato sauce

Salt and pepper to taste

PER SERVING:
Calories: 400
Protein (g): 35.2
Carbohydrates (g): 27.7
Fat (g): 18.4
Saturated Fat (g): 2.5
Cholesterol (mg): 45.2
Dietary Fiber (g): 6.5
Sodium (mg): 454

Heat oil to hot, but not smoking, over medium-high heat in a 12-inch non-stick skillet. Add garlic and onion. Cook, stirring, until onion is well-browned, about 6 minutes.

Stir in clam juice, sun-dried tomatoes, marjoram, and oregano. Raise heat and boil vigorously, uncovered, stirring once or twice, until liquid is reduced to about 2 tablespoons, about 4 minutes. Add fish and tomato sauce; simmer 3 to 5 minutes longer just until pieces are cooked through and flavors are well blended. Add salt and pepper if desired.

FISH STEW MARSALA

While marsala wine is often used in Italian recipes, it is not often paired with fish. However, it adds a distinctive, appealing note to this simple fish stew.

1½ tablespoons olive oil, preferably extra-virgin
1 large onion, chopped
1 cup coarsely chopped mixed red and green bell pepper
½ cup coarsely chopped celery
1 teaspoon minced garlic
2¼ cups reduced-sodium, *or* regular, chicken broth
⅓ cup dry marsala wine
1 teaspoon dried thyme leaves
2 cups medium-sized pasta shells, cooked barely *al dente* and drained
¼ cup tomato paste blended with ¼ cup water
2 tablespoons lemon juice
  Salt and pepper to taste
1 pound boneless, skinless haddock, *or* similar white fish, fillets,
  cut into large chunks

PREPARATION TIME:
15 minutes
COOKING TIME:
20 minutes
SERVINGS: *4*

In a 12-inch, deep-sided non-stick skillet or 13-inch saute pan over high heat, combine oil, onion, bell pepper, and celery. Reduce heat slightly, and cook, stirring, 3 minutes. Add garlic; cook until onion is browned, about 2 minutes longer. Add broth, marsala, and thyme.

Bring to a boil and cook, uncovered, for 10 minutes to reduce liquid. Stir in pasta, along with tomato paste mixture, lemon juice, and salt and pepper, if desired. Add fish; simmer 3 to 4 minutes until the pieces are opaque and flake when touched with a fork. Serve stew in large soup plates or bowls.

PER SERVING:
Calories: 427
Protein (g): 31.1
Carbohydrates (g): 52.3
Fat (g): 8.5
Saturated Fat (g): 1.4
Cholesterol (mg): 65.2
Dietary Fiber (g): 3.2
Sodium (mg): 244

vege

tarian and hearty vegetable dishes

Stuffed Artichoke Casserole

Italian Bean Pot

Eggplant Parmesan

Lasagne Casserole

Parmesan Polenta

Microwave Risotto and Peas

Microwave Risotto

Risotto with Celery and Roasted Peppers

Roasted Vegetables

Portobello Mushroom Sandwiches

STUFFED ARTICHOKE CASSEROLE

I've enjoyed stuffed artichokes in Italian restaurants from New York to California. This casserole, which makes a nice side dish, recreates the flavor combination with far less work.

PREPARATION TIME:
13 minutes
COOKING TIME:
5 minutes
SERVINGS: *5, side dish*

1   14–15-ounce can water-packed artichoke heart quarters, drained
1   tablespoon olive oil
1   large onion, chopped
½   teaspoon chopped garlic
⅔   cup reduced-sodium, *or* regular, chicken broth, divided
½   teaspoon dried oregano leaves
    Salt and pepper to taste
2   cups seasoned commercial cube-style stuffing

Remove and discard any tough outer leaves from artichokes. Cut artichokes into small slices. Set aside.

In a 2-quart microwave-safe casserole, combine oil, onion, garlic, and 3 tablespoons of broth. Cover with casserole lid, and microwave about 3 to 4 minutes, on High power, stirring contents halfway through microwaving, until onion is tender. Stir in oregano and salt and pepper, if desired. Add stuffing and remaining broth. Stir to mix well. Stir in reserved artichokes, distributing evenly. Cover and microwave on High power an additional 2 to 4 minutes or until stuffing is heated through.

HELPFUL HINT:

If it's more convenient, you can cook the vegetables in the microwave as directed above, but after adding the artichokes, bake the casserole in a 375-degree oven for 20 to 25 minutes. Make sure your casserole is ovenproof.

PER SERVING:
Calories: 130
Protein (g): 4.3
Carbohydrates (g): 19.6
Fat (g): 3.6
Saturated Fat (g): 0.6
Cholesterol (mg): 0.2
Dietary Fiber (g): 1.1
Sodium (mg): 449

ITALIAN BEAN POT

Because this bean pot is cooked in the microwave, it's ready in a snap. I serve it as a side dish or as a vegetarian main dish.

PREPARATION TIME:
15 minutes
COOKING TIME:
12 minutes
SERVINGS: *8, side dish*

½ cup dry-packed sun-dried tomatoes
1 medium-sized onion, chopped
1½ cups diced zucchini
½ teaspoon minced garlic
1 tablespoon olive oil
2 19-ounce cans cannellini beans, rinsed and drained
1 14½-ounce can Italian-seasoned diced tomatoes
1 8-ounce can tomato sauce
Salt and pepper to taste

In a small bowl, pour boiling water over sun-dried tomatoes and allow to soak for 8 to 10 minutes. Drain and cut into quarters. Set aside.

Meanwhile, in a 2½-quart microwave-safe casserole, combine onion, zucchini, garlic, oil, and 2 tablespoons of water. Cover with casserole lid, and microwave on High power about 6 or 7 minutes or until onion is tender; stop and stir once during microwaving.

Add beans, reserved sun-dried tomatoes, diced tomatoes, tomato sauce, and salt and pepper, if desired. Cover and microwave about 6 or 7 minutes or until flavors are well blended; stop and stir once during microwaving.

PER SERVING:
Calories: 157
Protein (g): 7
Carbohydrates (g): 27.3
Fat (g): 2.4
Saturated Fat (g): 0.3
Cholesterol (mg): 0
Dietary Fiber (g): 6.9
Sodium (mg): 778

EGGPLANT PARMESAN

Although the eggplant slices are fried in most versions of this Italian classic, baking is easier and healthier and yields equally tasty results. If time is short, a good-quality meatless commercial pasta sauce may be substituted for one of the homemade pasta sauces in this book.

PREPARATION TIME:

18 minutes

COOKING TIME:

35 minutes

SERVINGS: **9**

- 1 cup Italian-seasoned bread crumbs
- ¼ cup plus 1 tablespoon grated Parmesan, divided
- 2 medium-sized eggplants (about 2¼ pounds total), peeled and cut crosswise into ½-inch slices
- ⅔ cup liquid egg substitute, *or* 2 eggs beaten with 1 tablespoon water
- 3 cups homemade Marinara Sauce (see page 40), *or* meatless commercial pasta sauce
- 1½ cups shredded part-skim mozzarella cheese

Preheat oven to 475 degrees.

Coat a 12-inch by 18-inch or similar very large baking sheet with non-stick spray. Also spray a 3-quart flat rectangular casserole or lasagne pan with non-stick spray.

In a large, shallow bowl, stir together bread crumbs and ¼ cup Parmesan until well mixed. One at a time, dip eggplant slices into egg substitute, shaking off any excess. Then dip each eggplant slice into bread crumb mixture until evenly coated all over. Arrange slices, separated, on baking sheet.

Bake in upper third of oven until slices are nicely browned, 10 to 12 minutes. Turn with spatula and bake slices 8 to 10 minutes longer or until well browned. Set aside.

Spread about half of Marinara sauce in casserole. Using a spatula, transfer eggplant to casserole, overlapping slices slightly. Top with remaining sauce, then mozzarella, then remaining 1 tablespoon Parmesan.

Reset oven to 375 degrees. Bake until sauce is bubbly, about 15 minutes longer.

Not only is liquid egg substitute a good idea for cholesterol counters, but in this recipe it works just as well as whole eggs and has the advantage of being ready to pour and use. Some brands can be stored in the freezer and thawed in about a minute in a microwave oven, which also makes them very convenient when you run out of eggs.

PER SERVING:
Calories: 159
Protein (g): 10.1
Carbohydrates (g): 17.8
Fat (g): 5.8
Saturated Fat (g): 2.8
Cholesterol (mg): 13.1
Dietary Fiber (g): 3.7
Sodium (mg): 415

LASAGNE CASSEROLE

This recipe is one of my old favorites. I started making it when I discovered how easy it is to put together a lasagne-like casserole using smaller pasta shapes.

10 ounces elbow macaroni, *or* similar pasta shape
 2 15-ounce cans reduced-sodium, *or* regular, tomato sauce
 1 16-ounce bag frozen mixed pepper and onion stir-fry, slightly thawed
 1 teaspoon minced garlic
 1 tablespoon Italian seasoning
    Salt and pepper to taste
 1 15-ounce carton reduced-fat ricotta cheese
 2 cups loosely-packed, reduced-fat shredded mozzarella cheese, divided
 1/3 cup grated Parmesan cheese, divided

PREPARATION TIME:
15 minutes
COOKING TIME:
15 minutes
SERVINGS: **6–7**

Cook pasta according to package directions. Rinse and drain in a colander.

Transfer 1/3 of the pasta to a 3-quart microwave-safe casserole.

Meanwhile, in an 8-cup measure or similar bowl, combine tomato sauce, peppers and onions, garlic, Italian seasoning, and salt and pepper, if desired. Stir to mix well.

Mix together ricotta and mozzarella cheeses, reserving 1/4 cup mozzarella. Top pasta with half of the ricotta-mozzarella mixture, spreading it out evenly with the back of a large spoon. Sprinkle 1/3 of Parmesan evenly over cheese mixture. Add 1/3 of sauce, spreading evenly. Top with another layer of pasta, remaining half of ricotta-mozzarella mixture, and 1/3 of Parmesan. Top with a layer of sauce. Top with last of pasta, last of sauce, then remaining 1/3 of Parmesan and 1/4 cup mozzarella.

Cover and microwave on High power about 6 to 8 minutes or until sauce is bubbly.

HELPFUL HINT:

If you like, this casserole can be baked, uncovered, in a 375-degree oven for 37 to 43 minutes, until bubbly. If the casserole is baked in the oven, be sure it is ovenproof, and do not add the topping cheeses until the last 2 minutes of baking.

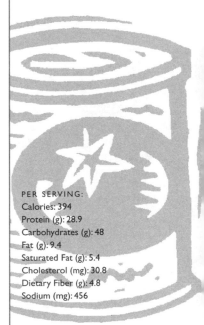

PER SERVING:
Calories: 394
Protein (g): 28.9
Carbohydrates (g): 48
Fat (g): 9.4
Saturated Fat (g): 5.4
Cholesterol (mg): 30.8
Dietary Fiber (g): 4.8
Sodium (mg): 456

PARMESAN POLENTA

Made from cornmeal, polenta was originally peasant food. Now it's often served in trendy restaurants. Sometimes it's a side dish; sometimes it's used as a substitute for pasta, with a sauce served over the top. This no-fuss version is made in the microwave. Try it with Tomato-Garlic Sauce on page 39.

PREPARATION TIME:
6 minutes
COOKING TIME:
15 minutes
SERVINGS: **4**

1 ⅓ cups yellow cornmeal
1 tablespoon granulated sugar
½ teaspoon salt, *or* to taste
3 cups water
1 cup 1% fat milk
1 medium onion, diced
¼ cup (1 ounce) grated Parmesan cheese

In a 3-quart microwave-safe casserole, combine cornmeal, sugar, salt, if desired, water, milk, and onion. Stir to mix well. Cook, uncovered, on High power about 8 to 9 minutes; stop and stir with a wire whisk after 3 minutes and 6 minutes. Stir again with a wire whisk until mixture is smooth.

Whisk in cheese. Cover with casserole top, and cook an additional 4 to 5 minutes on High power. Remove from microwave, and let stand an additional 2 or 3 minutes.

PER SERVING:
Calories: 223
Protein (g): 7.9
Carbohydrates (g): 41
Fat (g): 3.7
Saturated Fat (g): 1.6
Cholesterol (mg): 6.4
Dietary Fiber (g): 3.7
Sodium (mg): 139

MICROWAVE RISOTTO AND PEAS

Peas and rice are often served together in Venice. I've modified the recipe so that you can make it in the microwave—in a snap.

RISOTTO:

- ¾ cup uncooked arborio rice
- 2 tablespoons butter, *or* margarine
- 2⅔ cups reduced-sodium, *or* regular, chicken broth
- ¼ teaspoon dried thyme leaves

PEAS:

- 2 cups frozen green peas
- ¾ cup reduced-sodium, *or* regular, chicken broth
- ½ teaspoon chopped garlic
- ⅓ cup grated Parmesan cheese
  Salt and white pepper to taste

In a 2½-quart microwave-safe casserole, combine rice and butter. Microwave, uncovered, 60 seconds on High power. Stir well. Add broth and thyme. Stir to mix well. Cover with casserole lid, and microwave about 7 to 8 minutes. Stir well. Uncover and microwave an additional 11 to 13 minutes or until most of liquid is absorbed and rice is tender. Allow to stand 2 to 3 minutes.

While risotto is cooking, in a large saucepan, combine peas, broth, and garlic. Bring to a boil. Cover, turn off heat, and allow to sit on burner for 6 minutes.

When risotto is done, stir in peas. Stir in Parmesan. Add salt and pepper to taste, if desired. Allow to stand 2 to 3 minutes. Garnish with parsley sprigs, if desired.

HELPFUL HINT:

For extra color, add 2 tablespoons of chopped parsley to the peas before cooking them.

PREPARATION TIME:
8 minutes
COOKING TIME:
19 minutes
SERVINGS:
6–7, side dish

PER SERVING:
Calories: 176
Protein (g): 6.4
Carbohydrates (g): 23.7
Fat (g): 6.1
Saturated Fat (g): 3.4
Cholesterol (mg): 12.3
Dietary Fiber (g): 3.1
Sodium (mg): 166

MICROWAVE RISOTTO

In place of pasta, Italians sometimes serve risotto, which is made from arborio rice. The high starch content gives it a creamy texture. Here's a quick risotto recipe made in the microwave. Use it as a side dish, or serve it with any of the sauces in this book.

PREPARATION TIME:
5 minutes
COOKING TIME:
20 minutes
SERVINGS: **5–6, side dish**

- I cup uncooked arborio rice
- 3⅓ cups reduced-sodium, *or* regular, chicken broth, divided
- ¼ teaspoon white pepper
- ⅓ cup grated Parmesan cheese (optional)

In a 3-quart microwave-safe casserole or similar container, combine rice and 3 table-spoons broth. Microwave, uncovered, 60 seconds on High power. Stir well. Add remaining broth and pepper. Stir to mix well. Cover with casserole lid, and microwave about 8 to 9 minutes. Stir well.

Uncover and microwave an additional 9 to 11 minutes or until rice is tender. Allow to stand 2 to 3 minutes so that rice absorbs any remaining liquid. If serving as a side dish, stir in Parmesan cheese.

PER SERVING:
Calories: 136
Protein (g): 3.3
Carbohydrates (g): 26.4
Fat (g): 1.6
Saturated Fat (g): 0.6
Cholesterol (mg): 0
Dietary Fiber (g): 1
Sodium (mg): 23

RISOTTO WITH CELERY AND ROASTED PEPPERS

The rice used in risotto, called arborio rice, has short, rounded grains and a translucent appearance. It is very absorbent and starchy, which accounts for its creamy, almost pudding-like consistency. Arborio rice is sold in gourmet shops, the gourmet sections of some supermarkets, Italian markets, and by mail order firms. If necessary, you can substitute granza or paella rice, a somewhat similar short-grained rice sold in ethnic Spanish markets. American short-grained rice, on the other hand, will not yield satisfactory results.

Unlike many risottos, this colorful and tempting Venetian-style version doesn't need constant stirring during cooking. It makes a light, meatless entree or a savory accompaniment for all sorts of main dishes.

PREPARATION TIME:
12 minutes
COOKING TIME:
25 minutes
SERVINGS: *6, side dish*

1	tablespoon olive oil, preferably extra-virgin
2	teaspoons unsalted butter, *or* soft non-diet margarine
¾	cup finely chopped onions
1	teaspoon minced garlic
2½	cups diced celery
2¾–3½	cups reduced-sodium, *or* regular, chicken broth, *or* vegetable broth
¾	cup arborio rice
1	11-ounce jar roasted red sweet peppers, drained and chopped
⅛	teaspoon dried hot red pepper flakes
¼	cup grated Parmesan cheese
3	tablespoons tomato sauce

In a medium saucepan over medium-high heat, stir together oil, butter, onions, garlic, and celery. Cook, stirring, 7 or 8 minutes until onions are translucent and beginning to brown.

Add 2¾ cups broth; let come to a boil. Stir in rice, roasted sweet peppers, and hot pepper flakes. Adjust heat so mixture simmers gently. Cook, stirring occasionally, until rice is barely tender, 18 to 22 minutes. Add more broth if mixture begins to thicken; it should remain slightly soupy.

Stir in Parmesan and tomato sauce until well-blended, and serve.

PER SERVING:
Calories: 188
Protein (g): 4.7
Carbohydrates (g): 26
Fat (g): 6
Saturated Fat (g): 2.3
Cholesterol (mg): 6.3
Dietary Fiber (g): 2
Sodium (mg): 283

ROASTED VEGETABLES

This is one of my favorite winter side dishes. There's nothing like the crusty texture and oven-roasted flavor of these vegetables.

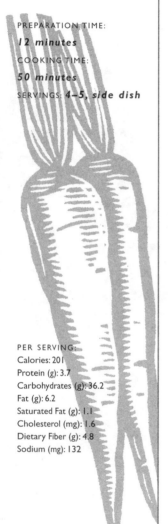

PREPARATION TIME:
12 minutes
COOKING TIME:
50 minutes
SERVINGS: *4–5, side dish*

4	medium onions, cut into small chunks
1¾	pounds (5 cups) thin-skinned potatoes, cut into 2-inch pieces
2	cups baby carrots
2	tablespoons olive oil
2	teaspoons Italian seasoning
	Salt and pepper to taste
2	tablespoons grated Parmesan cheese

Preheat oven to 450 degrees.

Combine onions, potatoes, and carrots in a large bowl. Toss with oil, Italian seasoning, and salt and pepper, if desired.

Transfer vegetables to a large non-stick, spray-coated baking pan or rimmed baking sheet, spreading them out evenly. Bake in preheated oven 45 to 50 minutes, stirring occasionally, until vegetables begin to brown and are almost tender. Sprinkle with Parmesan, and stir to mix well. Bake an additional 5 minutes.

PER SERVING:
Calories: 201
Protein (g): 3.7
Carbohydrates (g): 36.2
Fat (g): 6.2
Saturated Fat (g): 1.1
Cholesterol (mg): 1.6
Dietary Fiber (g): 4.8
Sodium (mg): 132

PORTOBELLO MUSHROOM SANDWICHES

Nobody will miss the meat in these savory sandwiches.

MARINADE AND MUSHROOMS:

- 2½ tablespoons *each* dry white wine and vegetable, *or* chicken, broth
- 2 teaspoons balsamic vinegar
- ½ teaspoon chopped garlic
- ¾ teaspoon *each* very finely chopped dried rosemary and dried thyme leaves
- ⅛ teaspoon (generous) *each* salt and pepper
- 2½ tablespoons extra-virgin olive oil
- 4 large portobello mushrooms (about 5 ounces each), stems removed

SANDWICH FIXINGS:

- 8 ½-inch-thick slices Italian bread
- 4 slices reduced-fat, *or* regular, provolone cheese
- 4 *each* lettuce leaves and tomato slices
  Bermuda onion and red bell pepper rings (optional)

PREPARATION AND MARINATION TIME:

45 minutes

COOKING TIME:

6 minutes

SERVINGS: **4**

In a small, deep, non-reactive bowl, whisk together wine, vinegar, garlic, rosemary, thyme, salt, and pepper until well blended. A few drops at a time, whisk oil into wine mixture until smoothly incorporated.

Place mushrooms, smooth sides up, in a flat, non-reactive dish just large enough to hold them. Pour ⅓ of marinade over them. Turn mushrooms stem sides up; pour over remaining marinade. Cover and refrigerate at least 30 minutes (and up to 8 hours if desired).

Preheat broiler to very hot, using highest setting. Adjust oven rack to about 4 inches from broiler element. Arrange mushroom caps, stem sides up, on a small, rimmed baking sheet. Drizzle any leftover marinade over caps, dividing equally among them.

Broil mushrooms for about 4 minutes on one side. Turn over and broil 2 or 3 minutes longer until cooked through.

Transfer mushrooms to a cutting board. Cut mushrooms into ¼-inch-thick slices holding knife on a diagonal. Lay provolone slices over 4 slices of bread. Immediately top cheese with hot sliced mushrooms, then tomato and lettuce slices, and finally onion and pepper rings, if desired. Top each sandwich with a second bread slice. Serve immediately, as the juice from the mushrooms will cause sandwiches to become soggy.

PER SERVING:
Calories: 375
Protein (g): 19.3
Carbohydrates (g): 37.6
Fat (g): 17.3
Saturated Fat (g): 5
Cholesterol (mg): 17
Dietary Fiber (g): 3.3
Sodium (mg): 605

vegetable side dishes

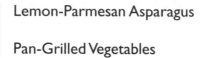

Lemon-Parmesan Asparagus

Pan-Grilled Vegetables

Crumb-Topped Tomato-Gremolata Bake

Zucchini-Mushroom Saute

Eggplant Skillet with Parsley

Braised Broccoli with Garlic Bread Crumbs

LEMON-PARMESAN ASPARAGUS

I love to serve this side dish in spring and early summer when the new crop of asparagus appears.

2	pounds fresh, untrimmed asparagus spears
2	tablespoons grated Parmesan cheese
2	tablespoons chicken broth
2	teaspoons olive oil
1½	teaspoons lemon juice
	Salt to taste
2–3	drops hot pepper sauce
1	tablespoon bread crumbs

PREPARATION TIME:

6 minutes

COOKING TIME:

3 minutes

SERVINGS: **8, side dish**

Wash asparagus well. Gently break off and discard tough white part at bottom of each spear. Lay spears in a large skillet, and cover with water. Cover skillet, and bring water to a boil over high heat. Reduce heat, and simmer 3 to 7 minutes or until spears are crisp-tender.

Meanwhile, in a small bowl, mix together cheese, broth, oil, lemon juice, salt to taste, and hot pepper sauce.

Transfer asparagus to a colander and drain well. Arrange on a serving platter. Drizzle cheese mixture over asparagus. Sprinkle with bread crumbs. Serve immediately.

HELPFUL HINT:

For the bread crumbs, use packaged Italian crumbs or crumb-style stuffing mix.

PER SERVING:
Calories: 45
Protein (g): 3.4
Carbohydrates (g): 5.2
Fat (g): 1.9
Saturated Fat (g): 0.5
Cholesterol (mg): 1
Dietary Fiber (g): 1.7
Sodium (mg): 58

PAN-GRILLED VEGETABLES

This quick and easy skillet vegetable dish makes a nice accompaniment to Turkey with Lemon-Caper Sauce (see page 139).

PREPARATION TIME:

10 minutes

COOKING TIME:

8 minutes

SERVINGS: *4–5, side dish*

2 teaspoons olive oil

1 large onion, sliced

½ teaspoon minced garlic

1 large red, *or* green, bell pepper, seeded and cut into strips

1 large zucchini, sliced, *or* 2 cups sliced cauliflower florets

½ teaspoon dried thyme leaves

Salt and pepper to taste

In a 12-inch non-stick skillet over medium-high heat, warm oil until hot but not smoking. Add onion, garlic, bell pepper, and zucchini or cauliflower. Sprinkle vegetables with thyme and salt and pepper, if desired.

Adjust heat so mixture cooks rapidly but does not burn. Cook, stirring frequently and breaking onion slices into rings, until slices are nicely browned and beginning to char slightly, 8 to 10 minutes.

PER SERVING:
Calories: 40
Protein (g): 1.1
Carbohydrates (g): 5.4
Fat (g): 2
Saturated Fat (g): 0.3
Cholesterol (mg): 0
Dietary Fiber (g): 1.5
Sodium (mg): 3

CRUMB-TOPPED TOMATO-GREMOLATA BAKE

An Italian seasoning mixture often sprinkled on vegetables, poultry, and seafood, gremolata usually features chopped fresh herbs—particularly parsley and garlic—and grated lemon zest.

Here, a sprightly, minty gremolata and a crispy bread-crumb-and-Parmesan topping make a succulent addition to baked tomato halves. This is a good side dish to serve with grilled or roasted meats.

Be sure to use vine-ripened tomatoes in this recipe.

PREPARATION TIME:

10 minutes

COOKING TIME:

18 minutes

SERVINGS: *6, side dish*

3 large vine-ripened tomatoes, cored and halved vertically
   Salt and pepper to taste
1 tablespoon olive oil, preferably extra-virgin
1 teaspoon minced garlic
1/4 cup finely chopped parsley leaves
2 tablespoons finely chopped fresh mint leaves
1/2 teaspoon grated lemon zest (yellow part of peel)
1/4 cup fine dry bread crumbs
1 1/2 tablespoons grated Parmesan cheese

Preheat oven to 425 degrees.

Set tomato halves, cut-sides up, in a flat, ovenproof dish large enough to hold them. Sprinkle salt and pepper over halves, if desired.

For gremolata: In a small bowl, stir together oil, garlic, parsley, mint, and lemon zest. Sprinkle gremolata over tomato halves, dividing it equally among them. Bake tomatoes on upper oven rack for 10 minutes.

For crumb topping: Meanwhile, in the bowl used for the gremolata, stir together bread crumbs and Parmesan. Sprinkle over baked tomatoes, dividing mixture equally among them. Bake 6 to 9 minutes longer until topping is golden brown and crispy. Remove dish from oven; let stand at least 5 minutes. Tomatoes may be served immediately or held for several hours. Reheat before serving.

PER SERVING:
Calories: 59
Protein (g): 1.7
Carbohydrates (g): 6.6
Fat (g): 3.1
Saturated Fat (g): 0.6
Cholesterol (mg): 1
Dietary Fiber (g): 0.9
Sodium (mg): 69

ZUCCHINI-MUSHROOM SAUTE

A light, mildly flavored side dish, this goes well with a wide variety of hearty Italian entrees.

PREPARATION TIME:
12 minutes
COOKING TIME:
12 minutes
SERVINGS: *6, side dish*

1	tablespoon olive oil
1	small onion, chopped
1½	cups coarsely sliced fresh mushrooms
½	teaspoon chopped garlic
4	medium (6½-inch) zucchini, cut into ½-inch cubes
¼	cup chicken broth, *or* vegetable broth
1	tablespoon finely chopped fresh basil, *or* ½ teaspoon dried basil leaves
	Salt and pepper to taste

In a 12-inch non-stick skillet over high heat, heat oil until hot but not smoking. Add onion and mushrooms. Adjust heat so mixture cooks rapidly but does not burn. Cook, stirring, 4 minutes. Add garlic; continue cooking until mushrooms are nicely browned, about 2 minutes longer.

Stir in zucchini, broth, basil, and salt and pepper, if desired. Cook, stirring frequently, until zucchini pieces are just tender, 6 to 9 minutes longer.

PER SERVING:
Calories: 43
Protein (g): 1.6
Carbohydrates (g): 4.6
Fat (g): 2.6
Saturated Fat (g): 0.4
Cholesterol (mg): 0
Dietary Fiber (g): 1.5
Sodium (mg): 45

EGGPLANT SKILLET WITH PARSLEY

Although preparation and ingredients are simple, this is a surprisingly savory dish. The recipe calls for microwaving the eggplant pieces before sauteing them. This cuts cooking time and unnecessary fat from the dish.

2 small eggplants (about 1¾ pounds), peeled and cut into ¾-inch cubes
1 tablespoon olive oil, preferably extra-virgin
1 medium onion, finely chopped
½ teaspoon minced garlic
¼ cup chopped fresh parsley leaves
1 tablespoon chopped fresh basil leaves, *or* 1 teaspoon dried basil leaves
1 teaspoon lemon juice combined with 2 teaspoons water
   Salt and pepper to taste

Spread eggplant in a large microwave-safe pie plate or serving plate. Sprinkle a tablespoon of water over eggplant. Cover plate with wax paper. Microwave on High power about 3 to 4 minutes, stirring after 2 minutes, until pieces are barely tender when tested with a fork. Turn out into a colander; drain well. Pat dry with paper towels.

In a 12-inch or larger non-stick saute pan or skillet, heat oil to hot, but not smoking, over high heat. Add eggplant, onion, and garlic. Adjust heat so mixture browns but does not burn. Cook, stirring, until pieces are nicely browned all over and tender, 6 to 8 minutes. Stir in parsley, basil, lemon juice–water mixture, and salt and pepper, if desired. Cook several minutes longer until piping hot.

PREPARATION TIME:
12 minutes
COOKING TIME:
12 minutes
SERVINGS: *5, side dish*

PER SERVING:
Calories: 80
Protein (g): 1.7
Carbohydrates (g): 13.1
Fat (g): 3.1
Saturated Fat (g): 0.4
Cholesterol (mg): 0
Dietary Fiber (g): 4.4
Sodium (mg): 7

BRAISED BROCCOLI WITH GARLIC BREAD CRUMBS

Toasted, garlic-infused bread crumbs add an appealing crunch to this dish. It should be served immediately as the crumbs lose their crispness and broccoli its bright color upon standing.

PREPARATION TIME:
6 minutes

COOKING TIME:
9 minutes

SERVINGS: **4, side dish**

PER SERVING:
Calories: 71
Protein (g): 3.5
Carbohydrates (g): 10
Fat (g): 2.7
Saturated Fat (g): 0.4
Cholesterol (mg): 0.1
Dietary Fiber (g): 2.9
Sodium (mg): 310

2 teaspoons extra-virgin olive oil, divided
2 large garlic cloves, peeled and smashed
3 tablespoons herb-seasoned bread crumbs
⅔ cup vegetable broth, *or* chicken broth
4 cups broccoli florets
1 teaspoon lemon juice combined with 1 teaspoon water
    Salt and pepper to taste

In a 12-inch or larger saute pan or skillet, heat 1 teaspoon of oil and garlic over medium-high heat. Adjust heat so garlic does not brown or burn, and cook several minutes, pressing on garlic to exude its juice. Discard garlic. Add bread crumbs; continue cooking, stirring, for several minutes more until crumbs are nicely browned. Remove crumbs from pan; reserve.

In the same pan, bring broth to a boil over medium-high heat. Add broccoli; simmer, stirring occasionally, until most liquid has evaporated and broccoli is crisp-tender, about 5 minutes. Stir in lemon juice and water, salt and pepper, if desired, and remaining teaspoon olive oil until broccoli is coated. Transfer broccoli to a serving bowl. Sprinkle crumbs over broccoli and serve.

HELPFUL HINT:

Herb-seasoned croutons or stuffing mix can be substituted for seasoned bread crumbs, if necessary. Simply seal the croutons in a small plastic bag and crush with a rolling pin until fine.

pizzas
and more

Easy Food Processor Pizza Dough

Pizza with Caramelized Onions and Smoked Turkey

Artichoke and Olive Pizza

Pepperoni Pizza

Peppers-Pepperoni Thick-Crust Skillet Pizza

Vegetable-Ham Thick-Crust Skillet Pizza

Spinach and Cheese Calzone

EASY FOOD PROCESSOR PIZZA DOUGH

Fresh, homemade dough makes a real difference in the taste of a pizza. If you have a bread machine, you probably already have a much-used recipe. If not, try this quick and easy food processor dough. Normally, hot tap water is the right temperature (115 to 125 degrees F.). But if your hot water setting is higher, let the water stand a few minutes before using it to avoid overheating the yeast.

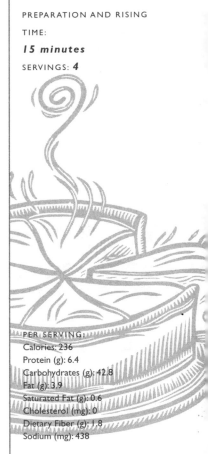

PREPARATION AND RISING

TIME:

15 minutes

SERVINGS: *4*

1¾ cups (approximately) all-purpose flour
1 package active dry yeast
¾ teaspoon salt
½ teaspoon granulated sugar
⅔ cup hot tap water
1 tablespoon olive oil

In food processor container fitted with a steel blade, combine flour, yeast, salt, and sugar. Pulse to mix.

Measure hot water from tap into a measuring cup. Add oil. With food processor on, gradually add water-oil mixture. Process until dough forms a ball, 5 to 10 seconds. Then process for 30 seconds longer to knead. If necessary, add additional flour through feed tube, a tablespoon at a time, until dough cleans sides of bowl. Remove lid; pat top of dough with a little olive oil. Replace lid and insert pusher tube. Let dough rise for 10 to 15 minutes.

Process for two or three pulses to punch down dough. Then carefully remove blade.

With lightly oiled hands, transfer dough to a non-stick, spray-coated pizza pan or baking sheet. For regular pizza, stretch and shape dough by hand or with a rolling pin into a 12-inch or 13-inch circle or an 11-inch by 14-inch rectangle.

Complete pizza with desired sauce, cheese, and toppings, and bake according to directions in individual recipe.

For skillet pizzas, follow directions in individual recipes that follow.

HELPFUL HINT:

To be sure the yeast rises properly, check the date on the packet to make certain it hasn't expired.

PER SERVING:
Calories: 236
Protein (g): 6.4
Carbohydrates (g): 42.8
Fat (g): 3.9
Saturated Fat (g): 0.6
Cholesterol (mg): 0
Dietary Fiber (g): 1.8
Sodium (mg): 438

PIZZA WITH CARAMELIZED ONIONS AND SMOKED TURKEY

Caramelized onions and smoked turkey make a wonderful pizza topping. Use either a purchased ready-made crust or one from the dairy case. Or try the homemade dough on page 119.

PREPARATION TIME:

7 minutes

COOKING TIME:

25 minutes

SERVINGS: **4**

1½ tablespoons butter
 2 cups thinly sliced onions
 ½ tablespoon granulated sugar
 3 ounces reduced-fat, *or* regular, deli smoked turkey, cut into thin strips
 1 large unbaked pizza crust
 ⅔ cup pizza sauce
 1 cup (loosely packed) shredded reduced-fat mozzarella cheese

Preheat oven to 450 degrees.

Melt butter in a 12-inch non-stick skillet over medium heat. Stir in onions and sugar. Cook, stirring frequently, until onions caramelize and turn light brown, 12 to 15 minutes. Add turkey and cook an additional minute, stirring, so that flavors blend. Remove from heat, and set aside.

If using homemade dough, roll out to a 12- or 13-inch circle or a 12 x 14-inch rectangle on a non-stick, spray-coated baking sheet. Or place purchased crust on baking sheet.

Spread pizza sauce evenly over crust, leaving a narrow line uncovered along outer edge. Sprinkle evenly with cheese. Distribute onions and turkey mixture evenly over pizza.

Bake in preheated oven 12 to 15 minutes (or according to package directions if a purchased crust is used) until edges of crust are browned. Cut into 8 wedges or rectangles.

HELPFUL HINT:

If you've traveled in Italy, you've noticed that many pizzerias, particularly those that do a high volume business, make their pizza in large sheets and sell individual portions in rectangles. So feel free to shape dough into a rectangle rather than a round; it's just as authentic.

PER SERVING:
Calories: 494
Protein (g): 28.7
Carbohydrates (g): 61.3
Fat (g): 16.6
Saturated Fat (g): 5.9
Cholesterol (mg): 36
Dietary Fiber (g): 2.1
Sodium (mg):1052

ARTICHOKE AND OLIVE PIZZA

If you like artichokes and olives, try them together as a pizza topping. Although the recipe calls for green olives, you may substitute black. For the crust, use the pizza dough on page 119, a pre-made pizza shell, or dough from the refrigerator case.

PREPARATION TIME:

6 minutes

COOKING TIME:

17 minutes

SERVINGS: **4**

 1 cup canned water-packed artichoke heart quarters, drained
 1 medium-sized onion, chopped
 ½ teaspoon minced garlic
 ⅔ cup pizza sauce
 1 large unbaked pizza crust
 8 medium green pimiento olives, sliced
 1 cup (loosely packed) shredded reduced-fat mozzarella cheese

Preheat oven to 450 degrees. Remove and discard coarse outer leaves from artichoke hearts. Set aside.

In a 1-cup microwave-safe measure or similar bowl, combine onion and garlic with 1 tablespoon water. Cover with wax paper, and microwave on High power about 2 minutes or until onion is softened. Drain.

Meanwhile spread sauce evenly over pizza crust, leaving a ¼-inch ring of crust exposed at outer edge. Spoon onion and garlic evenly over sauce. Add artichokes and olives, distributing them evenly. Sprinkle evenly with cheese.

Bake in preheated oven 15 to 17 minutes (or according to package directions if a purchased crust is used) until edges of crust are browned. Cut into 8 wedges.

PER SERVING:
Calories: 455
Protein (g): 25
Carbohydrates (g): 60.5
Fat (g): 13.5
Saturated Fat (g): 3
Cholesterol (mg): 23.7
Dietary Fiber (g): 1.4
Sodium (mg): 1284

PEPPERONI PIZZA

In this recipe, instead of sprinkling pepperoni on top of the pizza, I've cooked it in the sauce, giving the whole pizza a richer flavor. Make the pizza with the dough on page 119 or use a purchased crust.

PREPARATION TIME:
6 minutes
COOKING TIME:
22 minutes
SERVINGS: **4**

3 ounces pepperoni, cut into small pieces
1 medium onion, chopped
½ teaspoon chopped garlic
1 cup Italian-seasoned tomato sauce
  Salt and pepper to taste
1 large pizza crust (12–13-inch round; or 12 x 14-inch rectangle)
¾ cup (loosely packed) shredded reduced-fat mozzarella cheese

Preheat oven to 425 degrees.

In a 10-inch non-stick skillet, combine pepperoni, onion, and garlic. Cook over medium heat, stirring frequently, until onion is tender, 5 to 6 minutes. Stir in tomato sauce and salt and pepper, if desired. Stir to mix. Cook over medium heat, stirring frequently, 2 minutes longer.

Spread sauce evenly over pizza crust, leaving a ¼-inch ring of crust exposed at outer edge. Sprinkle evenly with cheese. Bake in preheated oven 15 to 17 minutes (or according to package directions if a purchased crust is used) until edges of crust are browned. Cut into 8 wedges.

PER SERVING:
Calories: 498
Protein (g): 26.1
Carbohydrates (g): 57.8
Fat (g): 19.8
Saturated Fat (g): 5.7
Cholesterol (mg): 36.7
Dietary Fiber (g): 1.7
Sodium (mg): 1532

PEPPERS-PEPPERONI THICK-CRUST SKILLET PIZZA

Red bell peppers lend bright color and flavor to this homey, thick-crust pizza. A small amount of pepperoni also adds zip.

This recipe calls for preparing the Easy Food Processor Pizza Dough on page 119. The resulting crust is so tasty and crisp that it's well worth the extra few minutes required.

PREPARATION TIME:
20 minutes
COOKING TIME:
25 minutes
SERVINGS: **6**

1	recipe Easy Food Processor Pizza Dough (see page 119)
1½	tablespoons olive oil, divided
1	medium onion, cut into coarse shreds
1	large red bell pepper, seeded and cut into 3-inch by ⅛-inch strips
½	teaspoon dried oregano leaves
2–3	ounces large pepperoni slices, cut into 1½-inch shreds
1	cup bottled pizza sauce, *or* tomato sauce
1	cup shredded part-skim mozzarella cheese

Prepare pizza dough and set aside to rise as directed in recipe.

Preheat oven to 450 degrees.

Combine 1 tablespoon oil, onion, and pepper in a 12- to 13-inch cast iron skillet or metal-handled non-stick skillet over high heat. Adjust heat so vegetables cook briskly but do not burn. Cook, stirring, until they begin to soften, about 3 minutes. Add oregano, pepperoni, and pizza sauce; cook, stirring, 2 minutes longer. Turn out mixture into a bowl.

Let skillet stand until cool enough to handle. Wipe out with a paper towel. Rub with a little of remaining ½ tablespoon olive oil.

Punch down the pizza dough. With lightly oiled hands, press dough into the skillet in an evenly thick layer. Rub dough with remaining oil. Spread vegetable-sauce mixture evenly over dough.

Bake on center oven rack at 450 degrees for 15 minutes. Sprinkle mozzarella cheese evenly over pizza. Continue baking about 5 minutes longer until dough is puffed, brown, and baked through and cheese is melted.

HELPFUL HINT:

If you need a vegetarian pizza recipe, the pepperoni can be omitted with good results.

PER SERVING:
Calories: 313
Protein (g): 11.9
Carbohydrates (g): 35.1
Fat (g): 13.6
Saturated Fat (g): 4.3
Cholesterol (mg): 18.4
Dietary Fiber (g): 2.7
Sodium (mg): 593

VEGETABLE-HAM THICK-CRUST SKILLET PIZZA

Assorted mushrooms, fresh tomatoes, ham, and imported black olives go together nicely in this rustic skillet pizza. You will need a batch of homemade pizza dough for this recipe (see page 119).

PREPARATION TIME:

20 minutes

COOKING TIME:

25 minutes

SERVINGS: **6**

1	recipe Easy Food Processor Pizza Dough (see page 119)
1½	tablespoons olive oil, divided
8	ounces mixed mushrooms (regular, portobello, porcini, etc.), coarsely sliced
3–4	green onions, including tender tops, coarsely chopped
1	teaspoon dried thyme leaves
1	teaspoon minced garlic
3–4	ounces lean smoked ham, diced
¾	cup diced fresh tomato
3	tablespoons pitted and chopped brine-cured black olives
¼	teaspoon *each* salt and pepper, *or* to taste
1	cup shredded part-skim mozzarella cheese

Prepare pizza dough and set aside to rise as directed in recipe.

Preheat oven to 450 degrees.

Combine 1 tablespoon oil, mushrooms, and green onions in a 12- to 13-inch cast iron skillet or metal-handled non-stick skillet over high heat. Adjust heat so vegetables cook briskly but do not burn. Cook, stirring, until they begin to soften, about 3 minutes. Add thyme, garlic, and ham. Cook, stirring, 2 minutes longer. Stir in tomatoes, olives, and salt and pepper. Turn out mixture into a bowl.

Let skillet stand until cool enough to handle. Wipe out with a paper towel. Rub with a little of remaining ½ tablespoon olive oil.

Punch down the pizza dough. With lightly oiled hands, press dough into the skillet in an evenly thick layer. Rub dough with remaining oil. Spread vegetable-ham mixture evenly over dough.

Bake on center oven rack at 450 degrees for 15 minutes. Sprinkle mozzarella cheese evenly over pizza. Continue baking about 5 minutes longer until dough is puffed, brown, and baked through and cheese is melted.

HELPFUL HINT:

If using a non-stick skillet, be sure it has a metal handle so it can withstand high oven temperatures. Most "heat-resistant" plastic, or phenolic, handles on pans are not designed for oven temperatures higher than 350-375 degrees.

PER SERVING:
Calories: 282
Protein (g): 12.6
Carbohydrates (g): 33.5
Fat (g): 11.3
Saturated Fat (g): 3.2
Cholesterol (mg): 18.5
Dietary Fiber (g): 2.2
Sodium (mg): 742

SPINACH AND CHEESE CALZONE

Calzone, Italian pocket sandwiches, are fun to make at home when you use refrigerator pizza dough and this easy cheese and spinach filling.

- ½ cup reduced-fat ricotta cheese
- 1¼ cups shredded reduced-fat mozzarella cheese
- ¼ cup grated Parmesan cheese
- 1¼ teaspoons Italian seasoning
- ½ teaspoon minced garlic
- ⅛ teaspoon salt (optional)
- 1 cup loose-leaf frozen spinach
- 1 10-ounce package refrigerator-case pizza dough

Preheat oven to 375 degrees. Spray a large baking sheet with non-stick spray.

In a large bowl, stir together ricotta, mozzarella, Parmesan, Italian seasoning, garlic, and salt, if desired. Break up any large lumps of spinach, if necessary. Stir spinach into cheese mixture.

Carefully unroll the pizza dough directly onto baking sheet, pressing it out with your fingers to make a 13-inch by 13-inch square, being careful not to tear dough. Cut square in half diagonally to form two triangles.

For each calzone, spoon half of filling mixture onto one-half of a dough triangle, spreading it evenly to about ½ inch from the edges. Moisten edges of dough with water. Fold dough over filling to make a triangular envelope. Seal by pressing with fork tines. Repeat with second dough triangle.

Prick top of each calzone with a fork to allow steam to escape. Spray top with non-stick spray. Bake for 15 to 20 minutes on center oven rack or until crust is lightly browned. Allow calzone to cool 3 or 4 minutes. Cut each trangle in half to make 4 servings.

PREPARATION TIME:
20 minutes
COOKING TIME:
20 minutes
SERVINGS: **4**

PER SERVING:
Calories: 352
Protein (g): 25.5
Carbohydrates (g): 38.4
Fat (g): 11.3
Saturated Fat (g): 5.8
Cholesterol (mg): 28.1
Dietary Fiber (g): 5.4
Sodium (mg): 837

presto
recipes

CHICKEN WITH ONIONS AND PEPPERS

Here's a chicken and pepper skillet that's quick and tasty.

- 1 tablespoon olive oil
- 1 pound boneless, skinless chicken breast meat, cut into large pieces
- ½ teaspoon chopped garlic
- 2 cups frozen mixed pepper and onion stir-fry
- 1 15-ounce can chunky, Italian-seasoned tomato sauce
  Black pepper to taste
- 2 tablespoons grated Parmesan cheese

In a large non-stick skillet, combine oil, chicken, and garlic. Cook over medium heat, stirring frequently, until chicken begins to brown, 4 to 5 minutes.

Push chicken to side of pan, and add peppers and onions. Cook, stirring frequently, 3 to 4 minutes, until peppers soften. Add tomato sauce and black pepper. Bring to a boil. Reduce heat, cover, and simmer about 12 minutes until chicken is cooked through. Serve over penne or similar pasta (not included in nutritional data). Sprinkle each serving with Parmesan cheese.

PREPARATION TIME:
5 minutes
COOKING TIME:
16 minutes
SERVINGS: **4**

PER SERVING:
Calories: 215
Protein (g): 28.5
Carbohydrates (g): 9.7
Fat (g): 7
Saturated Fat (g): 1.8
Cholesterol (mg): 71
Dietary Fiber (g): 2.8
Sodium (mg): 674

SAUSAGE AND PEPPERS SAUCE

Sausage gives this quick sauce instant pizzazz.

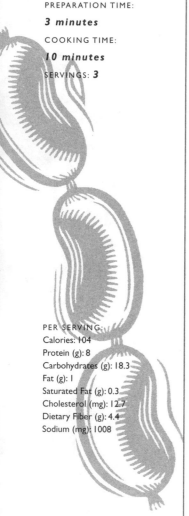

PREPARATION TIME:
3 minutes
COOKING TIME:
10 minutes
SERVINGS: **3**

3 cups frozen mixed pepper and onion stir-fry
1 15-ounce can chunky, Italian-seasoned tomato sauce
¼ cup reduced-sodium, *or* regular chicken broth
1 teaspoon granulated sugar
⅛ teaspoon black pepper, *or* to taste
3 ounces thinly sliced, precooked reduced-fat sausage (about 1 cup)
   Black pepper to taste

In a large saucepan, combine the pepper and onion mixture, tomato sauce, broth, sugar, and black pepper. Bring to a boil, reduce heat, and simmer, uncovered, about 5 minutes, stirring occasionally.

Add sausage and black pepper, if desired, and simmer for an additional 5 minutes, stirring occasionally. Serve over pasta.

PER SERVING:
Calories: 104
Protein (g): 8
Carbohydrates (g): 18.3
Fat (g): 1
Saturated Fat (g): 0.3
Cholesterol (mg): 12.7
Dietary Fiber (g): 4.4
Sodium (mg): 1008

SHRIMP WITH ARTICHOKES AND PEPPERS

This skillet dish is quick, easy, and brimming with flavor.

  1 14–15 ounce can water-packed artichoke heart quarters, drained
  1 tablespoon olive oil
  2 cups frozen mixed pepper and onion stir-fry
  1 teaspoon minced garlic
  1 15-ounce can chunky, Italian-seasoned tomato sauce
  3 tablespoons dry sherry
  1/8 teaspoon black pepper
  12 ounces medium-sized ready-to-cook shrimp
  8 ounces penne, *or* other similar pasta shape, cooked according to
      package directions

Remove and discard any tough outer leaves from artichokes. Set aside.

In a 12-inch non-stick skillet, combine oil, frozen peppers and onions, and garlic. Cook over medium heat, stirring frequently, 5 or 6 minutes until onions are tender. Add tomato sauce, sherry, artichokes, and black pepper. Stir to mix well. Bring to a boil, reduce heat, cover, and simmer 6 to 7 minutes until flavors are well blended.

Add shrimp; cover and simmer an additional 4 or 5 minutes until pink and curled. Serve individual portions of shrimp and vegetable mixture over pasta. Garnish with parsley, if desired.

HELPFUL HINT:

Although the recipe calls for dry sherry, you can substitute any dry white wine. If you don't have wine or sherry, you can use chicken broth.

PREPARATION TIME:
8 minutes
COOKING TIME:
15 minutes
SERVINGS: 4

PER SERVING:
Calories: 415
Protein (g): 29.7
Carbohydrates (g): 58.9
Fat (g): 5.3
Saturated Fat (g): 0.8
Cholesterol (mg): 166.1
Dietary Fiber (g): 4.7
Sodium (mg): 1007

FRESH BASIL-PARSLEY SAUCE WITH FETTUCCINE

The wonderful taste of this rich and creamy sauce comes from the fresh herbs. For a smooth texture, whisk the cheeses and milk as they cook.

PREPARATION TIME:

10 minutes

COOKING TIME:

5 minutes

SERVINGS: *4–5*

 4 ounces Neufchâtel cheese
 ¼ cup grated Parmesan cheese
 ¾ cup 2% fat, *or* whole, milk
 ⅓ cup *each* chopped fresh basil and parsley leaves
 ¼ cup thinly sliced green onion tops
    Salt and white pepper to taste
12 ounces cooked fettuccine

In a large saucepan, combine cheeses and milk. Cook over medium heat, whisking constantly, until cheese melts and mixture is smooth, about 2 minutes. Stir in basil, parsley, onions, and salt and pepper, if desired. Cook an additional 2 to 3 minutes to allow flavors to blend. Add fettuccine to sauce, and stir to coat well.

HELPFUL HINT:

This recipe calls for white pepper because it won't affect the appearance of the white sauce. If you don't have white pepper, the taste will be similar with black.

PER SERVING:
Calories: 290
Protein (g): 12.6
Carbohydrates (g): 39.1
Fat (g): 9.7
Saturated Fat (g): 4.6
Cholesterol (mg): 35.1
Dietary Fiber (g): 0.3
Sodium (mg): 198

ARTICHOKE AND RED PEPPERS SAUCE
OVER GARLIC FETTUCCINE

This creamy sauce, with its wonderful blend of flavors, is astonishingly easy to make. The only secret lies in using a wire whisk to smooth out the texture of the cheese and milk mixture as it cooks.

1	14–15 ounce can water-packed artichoke heart quarters, drained
1/4	cup coarsely chopped bottled roasted red peppers
4	ounces Neufchâtel cheese
1/4	cup grated Parmesan cheese
3/4	cup 2% fat, *or* whole, milk
1	teaspoon Italian seasoning
	Salt and pepper to taste
12	ounces cooked garlic fettuccine

Remove any coarse outer leaves from artichoke hearts. Chop hearts into large pieces. Combine with roasted red peppers, and set aside.

In a large saucepan, combine cheeses and milk. Cook over medium heat, whisking constantly, until cheese melts and mixture is smooth, about 2 minutes. Stir in Italian seasoning and reserved artichoke hearts and peppers. Stir in salt and pepper to taste.

Cook an additional 1 to 2 minutes. Stir fettuccine into sauce and serve.

HELPFUL HINT:

You can substitute chopped pimientos for the roasted red peppers, if you like.

PREPARATION TIME:
10 minutes
COOKING TIME:
18 minutes
SERVINGS: *4 to 5*

PER SERVING:
Calories: 320
Protein (g): 14.9
Carbohydrates (g): 43.9
Fat (g): 9.6
Saturated Fat (g): 4.6
Cholesterol (mg): 35.1
Dietary Fiber (g): 0
Sodium (mg): 399

QUICK TOMATO-OLIVE SAUCE

This fresh tomato sauce is a snap to fix. In winter, I make it with plum tomatoes. In summer, I use vine-ripened ones.

PREPARATION TIME:
12 minutes
COOKING TIME:
8–9 minutes
SERVINGS: *4 (3 cups)*

2 cups coarsely cut plum tomatoes
1½ cups diced red onion
1 large red bell pepper, seeded and chopped
20 pitted black olives, sliced
1½ tablespoons olive oil
¾ teaspoon *each* dried thyme and basil leaves
Salt and pepper to taste

In a non-stick skillet, combine tomatoes, onion, pepper, olives, oil, thyme, and basil. Cook over medium heat, stirring frequently, until onion is tender and tomatoes have softened, about 8 or 9 minutes. Add salt and pepper to taste, if desired.

Serve over pasta or polenta.

PER SERVING:
Calories: 139
Protein (g): 1.9
Carbohydrates (g): 13.5
Fat (g): 8.9
Saturated Fat (g): 0.8
Cholesterol (mg): 0
Dietary Fiber (g): 2.9
Sodium (mg): 237

PASTA POT

This quick and tasty stove-top dinner is made in one pot. I like to use a flavored pasta sauce such as "roasted red pepper and onion" or "garlic and basil."

2½ cups uncooked penne pasta
1 medium onion, coarsely chopped
3 cups mixed broccoli and cauliflower florets
1 26-ounce jar pasta sauce
⅓ cup grated Parmesan cheese

Bring 10 cups water to a boil in a small Dutch oven or similar large pot. Add pasta and onion, and cook 5 minutes. Add broccoli and cauliflower, and cook about 6 minutes longer or until pasta is tender.

Drain pasta and vegetables in a colander. Return mixture to pot in which it was cooked. Stir in sauce. Heat over low heat, stirring, until sauce is warmed, 1 or 2 minutes. Gradually add Parmesan, stirring to mix.

HELPFUL HINT:

You can substitute diced zucchini for all or part of the broccoli and/or cauliflower.

PREPARATION TIME:
6 minutes
COOKING TIME:
12 minutes
SERVINGS: **5**

PER SERVING:
Calories: 296
Protein (g): 13.2
Carbohydrates (g): 54.7
Fat (g): 2.7
Saturated Fat (g): 1.2
Cholesterol (mg): 4.2
Dietary Fiber (g): 6.1
Sodium (mg): 624

PEPPERONI POT

This easy and delicious stove-top dinner gets its rich taste from pepperoni. Since this sausage is so flavorful, you only need to use a little.

PREPARATION TIME:
6 minutes
COOKING TIME:
13 minutes
SERVINGS: *5*

2½ cups uncooked penne pasta
1 medium onion, coarsely chopped
1 teaspoon chopped garlic
4 ounces pepperoni
1 26-ounce jar pasta sauce

Bring 10 cups water to a boil in a small Dutch oven or similar large pot. Add pasta, onion, and garlic, and cook 9 to 11 minutes or until pasta is tender.

Meanwhile, thinly slice pepperoni, and cut each slice into quarters. In a medium skillet, quickly cook pepperoni over medium heat, stirring frequently, until sausage is lightly cooked, 2 to 3 minutes. Turn out pepperoni onto paper towels to absorb excess grease.

Drain pasta and vegetables in a colander. Return mixture to pot in which it was cooked. Stir in sauce and pepperoni. Heat over low heat, stirring, until sauce is warmed, 1 or 2 minutes.

PER SERVING:
Calories: 369
Protein (g): 14.3
Carbohydrates (g): 52.5
Fat (g): 10.9
Saturated Fat (g): 3.8
Cholesterol (mg): 17.9
Dietary Fiber (g): 4.3
Sodium (mg): 974

TURKEY WITH LEMON-CAPER SAUCE

In Italy, this dish would be made with veal cutlets. I've substituted turkey to reduce the cost and the cooking time. The delicate combination of lemon and capers works well with the turkey.

1 pound turkey cutlets

2 tablespoons white flour

$1/4$ teaspoon dried thyme leaves

   Salt and pepper to taste

1 tablespoon olive oil, divided

$1/2$ teaspoon minced garlic, divided

1 cup reduced-sodium, *or* regular, chicken broth

2 teaspoons lemon juice

1 tablespoon capers

Preheat oven to 200 degrees.

Place cutlets on wax paper. Dust with half of flour. Turn and dust with remaining flour. Sprinkle thyme, and salt and pepper, if desired, evenly over cutlets.

In a 12-inch non-stick skillet, combine one-half of oil and garlic. Add half of cutlets. Over medium-high heat, cook on one side until lightly browned, about $1\frac{1}{2}$ minutes. Turn over and cook on second side until lightly browned and just cooked through, about 2 minutes longer. Remove and reserve in shallow, ovenproof casserole. Cover and let stand in oven. Add remaining oil and garlic to skillet. Add remaining cutlets, and repeat cooking process. Transfer cutlets to oven.

Stir broth and lemon juice into skillet. Stir in capers. Cook over high heat, stirring, until liquid is reduced by half. Pour mixture over cutlets. Garnish with parsley, if desired. Or serve turkey and sauce on a bed of pasta.

PREPARATION TIME:
8 minutes
COOKING TIME:
9–10 minutes
SERVINGS: *4*

PER SERVING:
Calories: 155
Protein (g): 20.3
Carbohydrates (g): 3.4
Fat (g): 6.1
Saturated Fat (g): 1.4
Cholesterol (mg): 44.7
Dietary Fiber (g): 0.2
Sodium (mg): 131

CHICKEN CAESAR SANDWICH

Here are all the components of Caesar salad—in sandwich form. Although it's not a traditional ingredient, sliced tomato makes a nice addition to these sandwiches.

PREPARATION TIME:
5 minutes
COOKING TIME:
10–12 minutes
SERVINGS: *4*

8 large slices Italian bread

½ cup Caesar dressing (see Caesar Salad, page 16, *or* use purchased dressing), divided

4 boneless, skinless chicken breast halves

2 tablespoons grated Parmesan cheese

8 romaine lettuce leaves, washed, dried, and torn to fit bread slices

Adjust oven rack to 3 inches below the broiler. Preheat broiler.

Lay bread slices on a non-stick, spray-coated baking sheet. With the back of a spoon, spread a scant 1 tablespoon of dressing on one side of each bread slice. Toast slices until they begin to brown, 1 to 1½ minutes. Turn and toast the other side of each slice. Remove from broiler, and set aside.

Coat chicken with remaining dressing. Arrange chicken on a broiler pan. Grill 4 to 5 minutes on one side or until chicken begins to brown. Turn and grill other side until it begins to brown, 4 to 5 minutes. Remove chicken from broiler. Sprinkle with Parmesan cheese, dividing evenly among chicken pieces.

For each sandwich, place a chicken piece on a piece of bread, dressing side up. Top with lettuce and another bread slice, dressing side down. Serve at once.

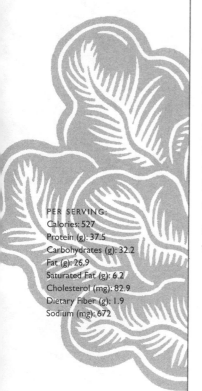

PER SERVING:
Calories: 527
Protein (g): 37.5
Carbohydrates (g): 32.2
Fat (g): 26.9
Saturated Fat (g): 6.2
Cholesterol (mg): 82.9
Dietary Fiber (g): 1.9
Sodium (mg): 672

PIZZA SANDWICH

Here's the quickest and easiest pizza you ever made—served open face on Italian or French bread.

- 1 unsliced loaf Italian, *or* French, bread
- ½ cup pizza sauce
- ½ cup shredded part-skim mozzarella cheese
- 2 tablespoons grated Parmesan cheese
  Toppings of your choice: chopped artichoke, slivered ham, roasted red bell peppers, sliced olives, etc.

Slice bread loaf in half lengthwise, and cut each half into 2 sections to form 4 serving-size pieces. (If directions call for "baking" bread, bake according to package instructions.)

Spread sauce evenly on bread pieces. Sprinkle evenly with mozzarella and then Parmesan cheese. Add desired toppings (not included in nutritional data). Heat in the toaster oven (in batches, if necessary) or under the broiler just until cheese melts.

PREPARATION TIME:

5 minutes

COOKING TIME:

1–2 minutes

SERVINGS: **4**

PER SERVING:
Calories: 370
Protein (g): 15
Carbohydrates (g): 59.2
Fat (g): 7.5
Saturated Fat (g): 2.9
Cholesterol (mg): 10.2
Dietary Fiber (g): 3.6
Sodium (mg): 949

TUNA PAN BAGNA

This is a delicious tuna sandwich, Mediterranean style! The tuna is tossed together with a savory dressing, then spooned over bread. The bread absorbs some of the seasoning mixture, which gives the sandwich its name— pan bagna, or bathed bread.

PREPARATION TIME:
10 minutes
CHILLING TIME:
10 minutes
SERVINGS: *3*

2 6-ounce cans solid white water-packed tuna, well-drained
½ cup coarsely chopped bottled roasted red peppers, well-drained
3 tablespoons well-drained capers
3 tablespoons extra-virgin olive oil
2 tablespoons balsamic vinegar, *or* red wine vinegar
2 tablespoons chopped fresh chives, *or* green onions
   8-ounce loaf Italian bread, halved horizontally
   Romaine, escarole, *or* other lettuce leaves and tomato slices for garnish
   Red onion slices and drained bottled pepperoncini peppers (optional)

In a medium-sized bowl, toss together tuna, red peppers, capers, oil, vinegar, and chives. Spread evenly over bottom half of bread. Cover with tomato and lettuce, if desired. Top with onions and peppers, if desired. Cover with remaining half of bread.

Wrap tightly in plastic wrap, pressing down to compact sandwich. Refrigerate about 10 minutes to chill slightly and allow flavors to mingle. (Or may be refrigerated up to 8 hours.) Cut into thirds and serve.

PER SERVING:
Calories: 494
Protein (g): 33.5
Carbohydrates (g): 41.9
Fat (g): 19.5
Saturated Fat (g): 3.4
Cholesterol (mg): 47.6
Dietary Fiber (g): 2.1
Sodium (mg): 1245

desserts
italiano

Fruit Pizza

Tiramisu

Cannoli Cake

Zuppa Inglese

Lemon Granita

Bread and Apple Pudding with Red Wine

Ricotta Cheesecake

Pear-Almond Cake

Almond Biscotti

Chocolate Meringue Cookies

desserts italiano

FRUIT PIZZA

While this dessert is probably an American invention, it's fun and easy to prepare. And it makes a beautiful presentation.

1 package (1-pound 2-ounce) refrigerator sugar cookie roll dough
1 package (8 ounces) Neufchâtel cream cheese, at room temperature
2 tablespoons granulated sugar
1 teaspoon vanilla extract
3–4 cups mixed fresh fruit such as sliced bananas, strawberries, and peaches, and/or blueberries, grapes, kiwi
¼ cup apricot preserves
½ tablespoon water

PREPARATION TIME:
20 minutes
BAKING TIME:
15 minutes
SERVINGS: *12*

Preheat oven to 350 degrees. Freeze cookie dough for 20 to 25 minutes to make it easy to handle.

Spray a 12-inch-round rimmed pan with non-stick spray. Spray a rolling pin with non-stick spray. Roll out and press dough directly onto pan with fingers, forming a ⅛-inch-thick "pizza crust." Bake for 15 minutes or until lightly browned. Cool.

Meanwhile, mix together cream cheese, sugar, and vanilla. When crust is cool, spread with cream cheese mixture.

Arrange fruit on cream cheese in an attractive pattern, overlapping if desired.

In a 1-cup measure or similar microwave-safe bowl, combine preserves and water. Microwave on High power 30 seconds or until preserves are softened. Stir to mix. Lightly brush mixture over top of fruit with a pastry brush or your finger. Serve at once, or refrigerate 1 or 2 hours or up to 12 hours before serving.

HELPFUL HINT:

The easiest way to make the crust is to roll it into a 9- or 10-inch circle. Then use your fingers to press it to the edges of the pan. Using a pan with a rim will keep the cookie dough from expanding too much as it bakes.

PER SERVING:
Calories: 250
Protein (g): 3.7
Carbohydrates (g): 33
Fat (g): 11.9
Saturated Fat (g): 4.7
Cholesterol (mg): 24.6
Dietary Fiber (g): 1.1
Sodium (mg): 226

TIRAMISU

There are scores of recipes for tiramisu. Here's an easy one that's rich and sweet, yet it's lower in calories than many. To simplify preparation, I've used espresso made with instant granules.

PREPARATION TIME:

20 minutes

CHILLING TIME:

6 hours

SERVINGS: **15**

¾ cup espresso

1–2 tablespoons rum (optional)

1 15-ounce package reduced-fat ricotta cheese

8 ounces mascarpone cheese

4 ounces Neufchâtel cheese, cut into 4 chunks

2 tablespoons water

¾ cup powdered sugar

12 ounces ladyfingers

½ tablespoon cocoa powder

PER SERVING:
Calories: 236
Protein (g): 8.7
Carbohydrates (g): 21.6
Fat (g): 12.8
Saturated Fat (g): 6.6
Cholesterol (mg): 106.9
Dietary Fiber (g): 0.2
Sodium (mg): 109

Combine espresso and rum, if used, and set aside to cool slightly.

Meanwhile, in a food processor container, combine ricotta, mascarpone, Neufchâtel, and water. Process until smooth. With processor running, add sugar. Process until well combined.

Arrange half of ladyfingers in a 2-quart flat glass baking dish. Spoon half of espresso mixture over ladyfingers. Spoon half of cheese mixture over ladyfingers, spreading evenly.

Lay remaining ladyfingers over first layer. Spoon on remaining espresso mixture. Spoon remaining cheese mixture over ladyfingers.

Insert 6 to 8 toothpicks into top of tiramisu to keep plastic wrap from sticking to sauce. Cover with plastic wrap, and refrigerate until completely chilled and flavors are well blended, 6 hours or up to 24 hours. Before serving, sift cocoa powder over top of tiramisu.

CANNOLI CAKE

Cannolis are Italian pastry shells stuffed with a sweetened ricotta cheese filling. You can sometimes buy the shells in Italian specialty groceries. But it's easier simply to spread the filling on a slice of cake.

1½ cups reduced-fat ricotta cheese
½ cup powdered sugar
½ teaspoon vanilla extract
    Dash ground cinnamon
¼ cup semisweet mini-chocolate morsels
1 13–16-ounce reduced-fat pound cake, *or* other yellow *or* white cake,
    cut into 8 slices
    Toasted almonds, pine nuts, *or* chopped pistachio nuts (optional)

In a food processor, combine ricotta, sugar, vanilla, and cinnamon. Process until smooth. Transfer to a small bowl. Stir in chocolate. Filling can be made up to 24 hours in advance and refrigerated.

When ready to serve, spread about 3 tablespoons of filling on each slice of cake. Sprinkle with nuts, if desired.

PREPARATION TIME:
15 minutes
SERVINGS: *8*

PER SERVING:
Calories: 216
Protein (g): 8.9
Carbohydrates (g): 40.9
Fat (g): 2.7
Saturated Fat (g): 1.6
Cholesterol (mg): 8.1
Dietary Fiber (g): 0.5
Sodium (mg): 246

ZUPPA INGLESE

This rich-tasting and festive dessert makes a wonderful finale to a company meal. Although the custard must be prepared ahead, the dish is really quite easy. The recipe suggests using strawberries, blueberries, and peaches. However, you can substitute raspberries, pineapple, and kiwi fruit for an equally colorful combination. Or use other seasonal berries and fruit you have on hand.

PREPARATION TIME:

20 minutes

COOKING TIME:

9 minutes

CHILLING TIME:

several hours

SERVINGS: *8*

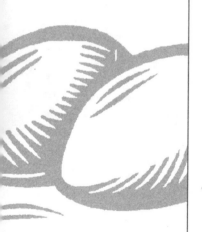

CUSTARD:

1	large egg white
1	large egg
2 ½	cups 2% fat milk
⅓	cup granulated sugar
¼	cup cornstarch
1	tablespoon butter, *or* margarine
1	tablespoon vanilla extract

FRUIT:

5	cups fresh fruit (a combination of blueberries, hulled and sliced strawberries, and/or peeled and sliced peaches)
⅓	cup granulated sugar
3	tablespoons rum, *or* fruit brandy

CAKE:

12	ounces ladyfingers

For Custard: In a 4-cup glass measure or similar microwave-safe bowl, beat together egg and egg white with a fork or wire whisk until smooth and frothy. Stir in milk. Cover with wax paper, and microwave on High power 2 ½ to 3 ½ minutes, stopping and stirring three times, until the mixture is hot but not boiling.

In the top of a double boiler, mix together sugar and cornstarch. Gradually beat in heated milk mixture, stirring vigorously and scraping the pan bottom until smooth.

Cook over boiling water, stirring vigorously, for 4 to 5 minutes or until mixture thickens. Remove from heat. Stir in butter and vanilla. Cover and refrigerate 3 or 4 hours or up to 48 hours.

For Fruit: Combine fruit in a medium bowl. Add sugar and rum. Stir to mix. Cover and refrigerate ½ hour.

To assemble: Arrange ⅓ of ladyfingers in large glass bowl with straight sides. Spoon ⅓ of fruit mixture over cake. Top with ⅓ of custard. Repeat layers, reserving ⅓ cup of fruit mixture for garnish. Arrange remaining fruit in center, atop dessert.

Cover and refrigerate several hours or up to 24 hours.

HELPFUL HINT:

If you don't want to make your own custard, you can use packaged vanilla pudding mix. If ladyfingers are unavailable, make the recipe with chunks of pound cake or angel food cake.

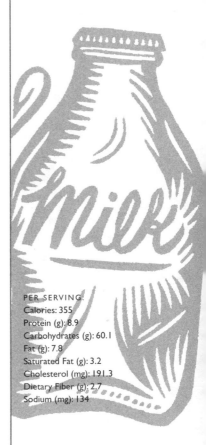

PER SERVING:
Calories: 355
Protein (g): 8.9
Carbohydrates (g): 60.1
Fat (g): 7.8
Saturated Fat (g): 3.2
Cholesterol (mg): 191.3
Dietary Fiber (g): 2.7
Sodium (mg): 134

LEMON GRANITA

This simple dessert boasts a wonderfully lemony tartness and taste and an icy, slushy consistency. It's reminiscent of the lemon ice sold at gelato shops all over Italy. Unlike sherbet, it does not require an ice cream maker.

PREPARATION TIME:

10 minutes

COOKING TIME:

4 minutes

CHILLING TIME:

4 hours

SERVINGS:

7 (scant 1 quart)

PER SERVING:
Calories: 88
Protein (g): 0.1
Carbohydrates (g): 23.4
Fat (g): 0
Saturated Fat (g): 0
Cholesterol (mg): 0
Dietary Fiber (g): 0.2
Sodium (mg): 3

$\frac{2}{3}$ cup fresh lemon juice

2 teaspoons very finely grated lemon zest (yellow part of skin)

2$\frac{3}{4}$ cups water

$\frac{2}{3}$–$\frac{3}{4}$ cup granulated sugar

1 tablespoon light corn syrup

Mint leaves for garnish (optional)

Combine juice and zest in a 1-cup measure; set aside.

Stir together water, $\frac{2}{3}$ cup sugar, and corn syrup in a medium-sized saucepan. Bring just to a boil over medium-high heat. Cover and gently boil 1$\frac{1}{2}$ minutes. Remove lid and continue boiling, without stirring, 2 minutes longer. Remove from heat; let stand until lukewarm. Stir lemon juice into sugar mixture. Stir in 1 tablespoon more sugar, if a slightly less tart granita is desired.

Pour mixture into a large, shallow, non-reactive container or bowl. Freeze for at least 4 hours, stirring mixture with a fork three or four times during freezing to break it up and form icy crystals. Just before serving, break up with a fork again. Serve granita piled into parfait glasses or sherbet dishes. Garnish with mint leaves, if desired.

Store in freezer (tightly covered) up to 4 days.

HELPFUL HINT:

For the intense, zesty flavor so characteristic of Italian ices, be sure to use fresh lemon juice and zest in this recipe.

BREAD AND APPLE PUDDING WITH RED WINE

Unless you're from northern Italy, this is not your mother's bread pudding. Instead of milk, the bread is moistened with wine. If you don't have stale bread, cube fresh Italian bread and lay it on a baking sheet for several hours at room temperature. Or bake the cubes at 210 degrees for 20 minutes, then turn off the oven, open the door, and let the cubes continue to dry out for 10 minutes.

PREPARATION TIME:

15 minutes

BAKING TIME:

40 minutes

SERVINGS: *12*

    1   cup chianti, *or other inexpensive red wine*
    ½   cup sugar
    ¼   teaspoon ground allspice
    4   cups cubed, slightly stale, white Italian bread
    3   cups peeled and diced apples (about 3 apples)
    ¾   cup dark, *or light*, raisins
    ¼   cup sliced, *or chopped*, almonds
    ¼   cup tub-style diet margarine

Coat a 2-quart rectangular baking dish with non-stick spray and set aside. Preheat oven to 350 degrees.

In a medium bowl, mix together the wine, sugar, and allspice until sugar dissolves; set aside.

In a large bowl, slowly pour the wine over the bread, stirring to coat as evenly as possible. Stir in the apples, raisins, and almonds.

Arrange half the mixture in the baking dish. Dot with half the margarine. Add the remaining bread mixture. Dot with the remaining margarine.

Bake for 40 minutes or until the top layer of bread has begun to brown. Serve warm. If desired, top with ice cream or vanilla yogurt.

PER SERVING:
Calories: 149
Protein (g): 1.6
Carbohydrates (g): 25.7
Fat (g): 3.7
Saturated Fat (g): 0.6
Cholesterol (mg): 0
Dietary Fiber (g): 1.7
Sodium (mg): 99

RICOTTA CHEESECAKE

Ricotta cheesecake has a firmer texture than New York deli-style. But it's equally flavorful. Serve it plain or with fresh fruit. For the crust, you can use the Almond Biscotti recipe (see page 156) or purchased cookies. Break cookies into small pieces; then process to fine crumbs with a food processor.

PREPARATION TIME:
20 minutes
BAKING TIME:
65 minutes
CHILLING TIME:
3 hours
SERVINGS: *10*

PER SERVING:
Calories: 262
Protein (g): 15.6
Carbohydrates (g): 29.4
Fat (g): 9.1
Saturated Fat (g): 5.1
Cholesterol (mg): 30.3
Dietary Fiber (g): 0.6
Sodium (mg): 274

3/4 cup biscotti crumbs (see headnote)
3 cups reduced-fat ricotta cheese
1/2 cup granulated sugar
1/2 cup liquid egg substitute
1/3 cup all-purpose white flour
1 tablespoon vanilla extract
Grated zest (yellow part of skin) from 1/2 lemon
1 8-ounce package Neufchâtel cream cheese, cut into 10 chunks
1/2 cup golden raisins
1 1/2 cups sliced large strawberries, *or* other fruit for garnish (optional)

Adjust oven rack to center of oven, and preheat to 350 degrees.

Spread biscotti crumbs in a 9-inch spray-coated non-stick springform pan.

In a food processor container, combine ricotta cheese, sugar, egg substitute, flour, vanilla, and lemon zest. Process 1 minute until smooth. Through feed tube, add chunks of cream cheese one at a time. Blend until smooth. Turn off processor. Stir in raisins.

Carefully spoon cheese mixture over crumb base, being careful not to disturb crumbs. Spread ricotta mixture out evenly with the back of a large spoon. Place springform pan on a baking sheet, and bake for 45 to 50 minutes in preheated oven until center of cake appears nearly set when shaken. Turn off oven. Leave cake in oven with door closed for an additional 20 minutes. Cool on a wire rack for 20 minutes. Loosen sides of cake by running a knife around inside edge of the pan. Remove springform. Refrigerate cake 3 or 4 hours or up to 48 hours before serving.

When cake has cooled, store covered with plastic wrap in refrigerator. Before serving, decorate outside edge of top with a ring of strawberry slices or other fruit, if desired.

PEAR-ALMOND CAKE

Canned pears and sliced almonds speed the preparation of this traditional Italian cake.

- 1   16-ounce can juice-packed pear halves, drained and coarsely diced
- 1⅔   cups all-purpose white flour
- 1½   teaspoons baking powder
- ¼   teaspoon salt
- ½   teaspoon ground ginger
- ⅔   cup granulated sugar
- ¼   cup softened butter
- 1   large egg
- 2   teaspoons vanilla extract
- ¾   teaspoon almond extract
- ⅔   cup 1% fat milk
- 2   tablespoons sliced unblanched almonds

Preheat oven to 375 degrees. Coat a 9½-inch (or similar) springform pan with non-stick cooking spray.

Blot the pears dry with paper towels and set aside.

Thoroughly stir together flour, baking powder, salt, and ginger in a medium bowl.

In a mixing bowl, with the mixer on medium speed, beat the sugar and butter until light and well blended. Beat in egg, vanilla, and almond extract. By hand, stir in dry ingredients until just thoroughly incorporated. Stir in milk. Stir in pears. Immediately spread the batter evenly in springform pan. Sprinkle with almonds.

Bake cake in center third of oven 28 to 32 minutes or until a toothpick inserted in cake center comes out clean. Let cool on wire rack. Serve at room temperature.

PREPARATION TIME:
20 minutes
BAKING TIME:
28 minutes
SERVINGS: **8**

PER SERVING:
Calories: 277
Protein (g): 4.8
Carbohydrates (g): 46.1
Fat (g): 8.2
Saturated Fat (g): 4.3
Cholesterol (mg): 43.7
Dietary Fiber (g): 1.9
Sodium (mg): 248

ALMOND BISCOTTI

Mild and crunchy crisp, these are great dunking cookies to serve with cappuccino or regular coffee.

PREPARATION TIME:
20 minutes
BAKING TIME:
46 minutes
SERVINGS: **35–40**
(*1 1/2 x 2 1/2-inch slice*)

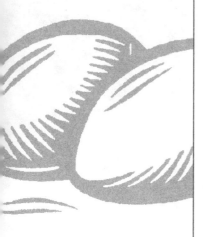

1/2 cup chopped blanched almonds, divided
1 cup granulated sugar
1 large egg
2 large egg whites
1 tablespoon lemon juice
Pinch very finely grated lemon zest (yellow part of peel),
  or 3 drops lemon extract
1 teaspoon almond extract
2 2/3 cups all-purpose white flour
1 teaspoon baking powder
1/4 teaspoon baking soda
1/8 teaspoon salt

Preheat oven to 350 degrees. Coat a 12 x 18-inch or similar very large baking sheet with non-stick cooking spray; set aside.

Spread almonds in a baking dish and toast, stirring several times, for 6 to 8 minutes until tinged with brown. Remove from oven; let stand until cooled.

Combine 1/3 cup toasted almonds and sugar in a food processor bowl. (Reserve remaining nuts for adding later.) Process continuously for several minutes or until almonds are ground to a crumbly meal. Add egg and whites, lemon juice and zest, and almond extract. Process until smoothly blended.

In a medium-sized bowl, thoroughly stir together flour, baking powder, baking soda, and salt. Turn out processed mixture into flour mixture. Add remaining chopped toasted almonds. Stir until mixed, using a large spoon. Then knead lightly with hands to form a smooth, cohesive dough. Divide dough in half.

With lightly oiled hands, shape each half into a smooth, evenly shaped, 2-inch wide by 12-inch long log. Smooth the surface by rolling each log back and forth on a clean work surface.

Transfer logs to a baking sheet, spacing at least 3 inches apart. Press down on logs to flatten slightly.

Bake logs for 25 minutes; their surface may crack. Remove pan from oven. Gently slide logs onto a cutting board. Using a serrated knife and working carefully, cut logs on a diagonal into ⅜-inch-thick slices. (If logs seem crumbly, let cool a few minutes before slicing.)

Lay slices flat on baking sheet. Return to oven. Toast for 15 to 20 minutes, stopping and turning slices halfway through, until they are just tinged with brown. (The longer the baking time, the crunchier and drier the slices.) Transfer slices to racks; let stand until completely cooled. Store airtight for up to 10 days. Freeze for longer storage.

PER SERVING:
Calories: 64
Protein (g): 1.5
Carbohydrates (g): 12.3
Fat (g): 1
Saturated Fat (g): 0.1
Cholesterol (mg): 5.3
Dietary Fiber (g): 0.4
Sodium (mg): 32

CHOCOLATE MERINGUE COOKIES

These are sweet, crisp-chewy meringue cookies with a full-bodied chocolate flavor. The meringue may gradually deflate upon standing, so be sure to form the cookies as soon as the batter is whipped. Also, use two baking sheets large enough to hold all the cookies at once, and bake both pans (staggered on two oven racks) at the same time.

You will need baking parchment for this recipe. Also, note that the recipe calls for unsweetened chocolate; semisweet can not be substituted.

PREPARATION TIME:
18 minutes
BAKING TIME:
50 minutes
SERVINGS: *45*
(2¹/₂-inch cookies)

¹/₄ cup unsweetened Dutch process (European-style) cocoa powder
1 ounce unsweetened chocolate, chopped
¹/₄ cup cornstarch
¹/₂ cup powdered sugar
4 large egg whites, at room temperature, completely free of yolk
¹/₄ teaspoon cream of tartar
Generous pinch of salt
1 cup granulated sugar
¹/₂ teaspoon instant coffee granules
1¹/₂ teaspoons vanilla extract

Preheat oven to 250 degrees. Line two 12 x 18-inch or other very large baking sheets with baking parchment.

Combine cocoa powder and chocolate in a food processor bowl. Process until chocolate is finely ground. In a medium-sized bowl, thoroughly stir together chocolate mixture, cornstarch, and powdered sugar.

In a completely grease-free large mixer bowl with mixer on High speed, beat egg whites until frothy and opaque. Add cream of tartar and salt; beat whites until soft peaks just begin to form. A bit at a time, add sugar, then coffee granules and vanilla. Scraping down bowl sides several times, continue to beat until mixture stands in stiff, glossy peaks. Using a rubber spatula, quickly fold chocolate mixture into whites until evenly incorporated.

Immediately drop batter by tablespoonfuls onto baking sheets, spacing about 1½ inches apart. Transfer pans to oven, staggering them on two racks in center half of oven.

Bake for 50 to 60 minutes or until cookies are firm on top, exchanging pans halfway through to ensure even baking. (Shorter baking time yields chewier cookies; longer time, crisper ones.) With cookies still attached to parchment, place on wire racks until thoroughly cooled. Carefully peel cookies from parchment.

Store cookies airtight for 3 or 4 days. Freeze for longer storage.

PER SERVING:
Calories: 32
Protein (g): 0.5
Carbohydrates (g): 7
Fat (g): 0.4
Saturated Fat (g): 0.2
Cholesterol (mg): 0
Dietary Fiber (g): 0.2
Sodium (mg): 5

index